STORM SHELTER

PROTECTING YOUR PERSONAL FINANCES

RON BLUE

This Billy Graham Evangelistic Association
special edition is published with permission from
Thomas Nelson Publishers.

THOMAS NELSON PUBLISHERS
Nashville • Atlanta • London • Vancouver

Other books by the author
Master Your Money
Master Your Money Workbook
Raising Money-Smart Kids
Taming the Money Monster
A Woman's Guide to Financial Peace of Mind

Published in Nashville, Tennessee, by Thomas Nelson, Inc., Publishers, and
distributed in Canada by Word Communications, Ltd., Richmond, British
Columbia.

The Bible version used in this publication is THE NEW KING JAMES
VERSION. Copyright © 1979, 1980, 1982, Thomas Nelson, Inc., Publishers.

Anecdotes and clients mentioned in this book are composites of actual
cases. Details and facts have been changed to protect identities.

Library of Congress Cataloging-in-Publication Data

Blue, Ron.
   Storm shelter / Ron Blue.
      p.   cm.
   ISBN 0-913367-70-2
   1. Finance, Personal.   2. Finance, Personal—Religious aspects-
-Christianity. I. Title.
HG179.B5655 1994
332.024—dc20   94–27610
                                                  CIP

Printed in the United States of America.

Contents

Acknowledgments

For an author, at least this author, finishing a book feels like a ten-thousand-pound gorilla has just been taken off my back. Writing acknowledgments is very close to the last step, and as I write I am sensing that the gorilla is getting ready to jump someplace else.

This book really needs to be characterized more as a project than a book because of the number of people who figured so significantly in its creation. Over the years, I have told audiences that everything I do is copyrighted; therefore, when you copy it, copy it right. I have meant that I don't believe I have ever truly created anything. I may have rephrased things or said them in a different or new way, but anything good that has been said or developed ultimately has its source in the truth. Not only that, but there are many others who could say it differently and probably better.

Completing this book humbles me because there were so many significant contributors. First of all, for the first time I have used a writer in the process. Jodie Berndt not only gave birth to this book during the last nine months, she also gave birth to her third daughter during that time. It has been a tremendous experience working with Jodie as she and I sat down to brainstorm, edit, rethink, and redo this book, chapter by chapter. She has challenged me where my thinking has been fuzzy or not right, and she has gently kept me on track with deadlines that were my responsibility. She has also maintained a far better attitude and perspective about the writing process than I have ever exhibited, and I really appreciate that beyond what words can say. To a very significant degree, this book bears her stamp as much as mine.

In addition to Jodie, three persons on my staff, Melanie Collier, Curt Knorr, and Fran LaMattina, have worked to make this book a success. Fran, our director of marketing, has coordinated much of the writing process. I have learned from her what a servant truly should be like. Curt, as director of our investment department, has created many of the illustrations and charts you will find in the last three chapters of the book. He also made sure we were credible and correct from a professional investment standpoint. Melanie dropped everything she was doing for the last three or four weeks of this project to draft and redraft my thoughts, coordinating tasks with Curt and Jodie to complete the last several chapters of the book. Melanie's contribution was beyond what I could expect of any of my staff members, and I deeply appreciate it.

Obviously, when someone like me, whose full-time job is leading and developing a growing business, works on a book, all of his or her staff pay a price for the time it takes to complete the project. I deeply appreciate my staff members' willingness to help in any way. Zoe Custer, my administrative assistant, once again has been a public relations jewel to all those who were trying to contact me over the last several months. As every day goes by, she becomes more irreplaceable.

I also want to acknowledge the team at Thomas Nelson—Janet Thoma, Brian Hampton, Amy Glass, and Sue Ann Jones—who would not stand for anything less than excellence. Thanks for keeping me on track.

And most importantly, to my wife, Judy, and to our family, you have once again graciously tolerated a tense and irritable husband and father as a book took shape and grew to completion. I am a man blessed beyond comprehension by the ones God has put in my life—my family and the staff at Ronald Blue & Co. As such, I go to bed every night thanking my Lord and Savior, Jesus Christ, for the privilege of serving Him in this temporal state called life.

Introduction

In August 1979 my wife, Judy, and I sat down over a hot-fudge sundae in an ice cream shop in Atlanta and discussed what we wanted to do vocationally for the rest of our lives. Judy had become a Christian in 1972, and through her testimony I had accepted Christ two years later. In 1977, deciding we wanted to devote our lives to full-time Christian work, we had left our hometown and the business I had started there and moved to Atlanta to accept a job with an Atlanta-based ministry. Now it was two years later, and we were taking a look at where our lives were heading.

My job with the ministry required frequent travel to various parts of the world, and each time I returned to the United States, I grew more impressed with how wealthy we are in America. The world has never seen a culture as financially blessed as ours. At the same time, though, my twelve years as an accountant had convinced me that, in general, Americans are incredibly fearful when it comes to thinking about and handling wealth.

On the back of a napkin in that ice cream shop, Judy

and I wrote down the priorities and goals we wanted to accomplish. Out of that evening came the beginnings of the firm I founded three months later. This firm's mission statement from day one has been this: to help individuals apply God's principles of stewardship in order to free up financial resources for the fulfillment of the Great Commission.

This mission is something I pursue with a passion. I have a vision to help Christians get a proper perspective on their finances to allow them to do what they really want to do—be the best possible stewards of the financial resources God has entrusted to them.

I recently read an interesting statistic from the Internal Revenue Service: As incomes go up in America, charitable giving as a percentage of income goes down. Surprisingly, the largest givers proportionately are those who earn less than ten thousand dollars per year. They give, on the average, 5.5 percent of their income, whereas those who earn more than five hundred thousand dollars per year give less than 3 percent of their income to charitable causes. Americans have often been characterized as the most generous people on earth. Why, in reality, are we so stingy?

I believe the answer to this question lies in the fear that grips our society. After talking to hundreds of people over the last fifteen years, I have realized an interesting correlation: The more money we have, the more we tend to worry about losing it. That fear is not without justification. However, I believe that in many cases it causes poor decision making when it comes to personal finances.

I have written this book out of a fifteen-year vision to communicate hope, encouragement, and freedom to those who will follow the biblical principles of planning and money management. I have a passion to see husbands and wives communicate about money and money management. I have a passion to challenge Christians who are leaders in their communities to be salt and light in a world that desperately needs examples of faith-based—as opposed to fear-based—decisions. I have a passion to make order out of what appears to be confusion. I know it is possible to achieve order in a world that appears to be confused because our God is not confused; nor does He author confusion.

Making or earning money is a lot easier than managing money. We tend to earn our money in a professional setting where we have been adequately trained and equipped. When it comes to handling our own money, though, we are in unfamiliar territory. Few of us have been schooled in financial management, and as a result, we either make mistakes, become fearful, or find it very difficult to make good decisions.

Also, I've observed that in many cases more money equals *less* freedom, not more. The logic behind this conclusion is that the more money you have, the more options you have, and consequently the more time and energy you must spend making decisions and managing your resources.

This book is about the perspective, paradigm, and plan you need to make wise choices and experience financial freedom. Because investment planning causes more fear than any other aspect of the financial-management picture, I have devoted the last three chapters of this book to helping you develop a practical and personal investment strategy.

This is not an investment or financial planning text-book. Rather, it is written as a book of encouragement to those who want to have the proper perspective, paradigm, and plan for managing the resources entrusted to them by God. By putting these principles into practice, we can look forward to standing before the Lord and hearing Him say, as He said to the faithful steward, "Well done, good and faithful servant; you have been faithful over a few things, I will make you ruler over many things. Enter into the joy of your lord" (Matt. 25:23).

PART

ONE

UNDERSTANDING ECONOMIC STORMS

Economic Uncertainty Is Certain

The picture is as clear in my mind today as it was nearly thirteen years ago. As I pulled off the interstate en route to my office, I did not see the road markers; instead, my eyes swam with the signs of the times.

The year was 1982. Interest and inflation rates had soared to all-time highs, investors faced crushing 70 percent tax brackets, and the price of gold leapfrogged daily. Taking stock of the situation, most analysts warned of a devastating financial explosion within the next few years.

As I drove to work that day, the economic consequences seemed both crippling and inevitable. I had just launched our investment and financial counseling firm. How, I wondered, were we supposed to respond to the clients who came to us for advice? Could anyone afford to purchase a home with 15 to 20 percent interest rates? Which kinds of investments and tax plans could stand up to double-digit inflation? And if the predicted monetary collapse did occur, would the resulting political turmoil uproot even the best-laid financial plans?

Suddenly, I felt the subconscious click of the proverbial lightbulb: The biblical principles of money management I had been teaching and using for years would work under any economic scenario. Armed with these concepts, I knew exactly how to help our clients weather the coming storm, no matter how hard the financial winds blew.

The predicted financial blowout never did occur. Yet as our business grew in the years that followed, we faced a thousand different financial situations that seemed specially tailored to test the worth and endurance of the money-management concepts our firm espoused. But in each and every case the biblical principles held fast, strengthening our clients' economic positions—and bringing them peace and security in the bargain.

> **Economic uncertainty need not spell disaster or upheaval in your personal finances.**

If you have not already discovered God's principles for sound money management, you soon will, for they serve as the very foundation for this book. Economic uncertainty need not spell disaster or upheaval in your personal finances. Nor should it foster anxiety, doubt, or gloom.

The first step in defeating uncertainty is to realize just how common—and normal—it is. In this chapter we will examine some of the major problems and questions that create uncertainty and threaten our sense of security. Typically, these are things we have little or no control over—yet their power to generate apprehension and fear is unmistakable.

Our preparedness for, and response to, economic change is vital to our ultimate success. Here and in the chapters to come, you will acquire the perspective and tools you need to triumph, no matter how severe the storm appears in the financial forecast.

THE WALLET WALLOP: THINGS THAT THREATEN OUR THRIVING

One of my fears as I navigated the interstate highway that day in 1982 was that we faced a "worst-ever" economic climate. Yet economic uncertainty—and its accompanying effects on our sense of security and well-being—are nothing new.

Ten years earlier, in 1972, we had been saddled with Watergate and an oil crisis that threatened to throttle the world's economy. Who can forget the lines at the gas stations or the rationing of fuel oil that winter? Then, too, I remember being hit with wage and price controls for the first time since World War II. And for the first time in my memory, the prime rate hit 10 percent. Economic security seemed an elusive, if not impossible, dream.

Economic uncertainty is nothing new.

Ten years before that, in 1962, the specter of economic and political uncertainty had hovered in every corner of the world. Our amazement at seeing a shoe-pounding Nikita Khrushchev vow to "bury" us turned to horror as the Cuban missile crisis unfolded. At that point a nuclear holocaust seemed at least possible, if not imminent. And Vietnam lay just around the corner. . . .

In 1952, in the shadow of the spread of Communism, amid the mud and blood of the Korean War, bomb shelters were among the best-selling items in the United States. In 1942 we faced Pearl Harbor and felt the full force of our entry into World War II. In 1932 we awoke to the nightmare of the Great Depression.

And on and on and on. The point is that we will always face uncertainty, and as we consider our finances, we need to plan from that perspective.

Ask someone on the street to identify the major causes of economic uncertainty today, and you are likely to get a laundry list of problems ranging from federal overspending to constantly changing tax laws. Concerns such as these are entirely legitimate. The federal budget deficit, inflation, tax-law changes, interest-rate shifts, and swings in the stock market are all valid reasons for concern and worry as we pinpoint some of the biggest threats to our economic security today.

The Budget Deficit

Alexander Hamilton was only thirty-four years old when George Washington appointed him secretary of the treasury. Yet Hamilton was a financial wizard, extremely well qualified for the job. His first priority was to bolster the national credit and with it, the public's confidence in their new government.

Most states were burdened by huge debts following the Revolutionary War, and Hamilton urged Congress to assume these obligations in full. Thus, as we took our first baby steps as a nation in 1790, we were saddled with a national debt of seventy-five million dollars—a staggering sum for a country still in its infancy!

Yet Hamilton was not concerned. He saw the national debt as a sort of communal blessing. The more folks the government owed money to, he reasoned, the more folks there would be who would have a personal stake in the success of the fledgling economy. Hamilton's ambitious plan, which provided for the debt repayment largely through new customs duties, breathed new life into the nation's postwar financial system—and turned the liability of debt into an unusual asset.

There was, undoubtedly, some wisdom in Hamilton's strategy—yet that was two hundred years ago. Today we would be hard pressed to characterize our national debt—which recently shot past the four-trillion-dollar mark—as a blessing. It doesn't matter who sits in the Oval Office or which party calls the shots in Congress, the deficit is not going to disappear anytime soon. As figure 1.1 indicates, our debt level has been climbing dramatically for two decades. Today, we are accumulating additional debt at the mind-boggling rate of more than thirteen thousand dollars per second!

The deficit is not going to disappear anytime soon.

The consequences of our national indebtedness parallel those of the family that continues to use credit cards and other debt to fund current living expenses. By obligating themselves to repay the debt at some point down the road, the family has mortgaged its future. The federal government, by continuing to spend more than its income, has done the same.

To grasp the full significance of the problem, imagine that the government stops overspending today. Furthermore, pretend that there is no longer any interest due on the amount that has already been overspent. Even with these concessions, if we were to attempt to repay the debt at a clip of one dollar per second, it would still take more than 128,000 years to dig our way out of the hole!

There are, of course, several options we could use to work our way back into the black. We could raise taxes—

an unpopular and historically impotent strategy. We could decrease spending—and tighten the belt on programs ranging from social security and health care to disaster relief and road construction. We could rely on inflation, stalling on debt repayment so we could repay our obligation in "cheaper dollars." Or we could let Congress repudiate the debt by passing a law declaring that we simply would not repay it.

None of these alternatives is entirely painless, and all

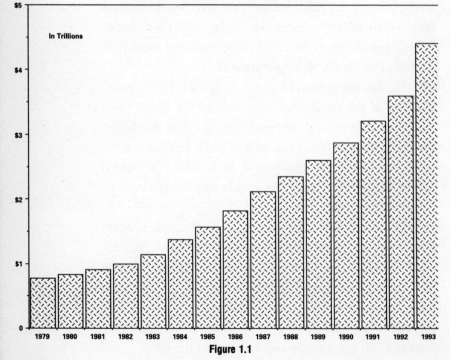

National Debt from 1979 to 1993

In Trillions

Figure 1.1

carry a tremendous economic, political, and even moral price. And as the deficit mushrooms, the future becomes less and less secure.

Inflation

Like the budget deficit, inflation affects both the strength of our national economy and our own personal financial planning. In 1968 my wife, Judy, and I purchased our first home in Dallas for twenty-five thousand dollars. We had just graduated from college—an education that cost us each about fifteen hundred dollars per year.

Had you told us then that in only twenty-five years, getting a college degree at some universities would cost as much as four times what we paid for that first home, we would have been shocked.

But that is exactly what has happened—thanks to inflation.

Today's inflation rate is around 3 percent. After experiencing 13 percent inflation in 1980, the 3 percent level seems quite acceptable. But it is not likely to last.

Figure 1.2 illustrates the volatile and unpredictable nature of inflation.

The net effect of inflation is to ultimately cheapen the dollar. In 1969, for example, if a dollar was worth one hundred cents, then by 1993 its value had dropped to only twenty-two cents—meaning we then had to spend five dollars to buy what had cost only one dollar two decades earlier.

In addition to the problems this creates for achieving financial goals, the very uncertainty of inflation makes accurate planning almost impossible. When we begin to talk in terms of inflated dollars, we start to feel

As the deficit mushrooms, the future becomes less and less secure.

The net effect of inflation is to ultimately cheapen the dollar.

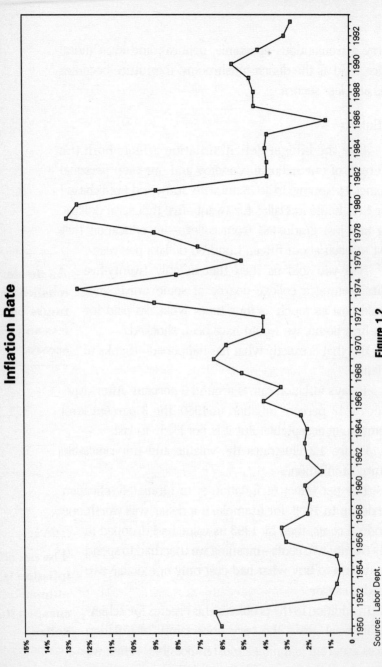

Inflation Rate

Figure 1.2

Source: Labor Dept.

overwhelmed. Contemplating the cost of retirement living, college education, or other long-term goals makes us want to throw up our hands and say, "There's just no way!"

Taxes

Suppose that, despite the specter of inflation, you have buckled down and developed a plan to fund college education for your two children. You know exactly how much you must put aside every month, and you have worked this into your budget.

Suddenly, the tax code changes—and with it, your cash flow. No longer are the dollars in your take-home pay adequate to meet all your budget demands. Now, to accommodate college savings, you must return to the budget worksheet and essentially begin from scratch.

The very uncertainty of inflation makes accurate planning almost impossible.

In my thirty years as a certified public accountant and financial counselor, I've seen the tax laws change annually. The entire tax code has been rewritten seven times in just the last twelve years: in 1981, 1982, 1983, 1986, 1987, 1990, and 1993. These dramatic shifts make long-term planning burdensome, if not impossible.

The uncertainty surrounding tax laws, coupled with a common distaste for paying taxes in general, has created at least two generations of poor tax planners. Most of us moan and groan as tax time approaches. Some under-withhold and anticipate a big "taxes-due" bill. Others overwithhold, giving the government a year's use of their hard-earned money, interest free.

April 15 comes around every year.

Neither of these is a desirable position, and neither represents good planning. April 15 comes around every year. Why not approach it from the vantage point of accurate annual planning—and avoid the tax-season surprise?

Stock Market Fluctuations

Wherever I speak, people always seem to ask me the same two questions: "I've owned X stock for five years. It's already doubled in value. Should I keep it or sell it?" and "My Aunt Mabel told me about a new company that's guaranteed to go up in value. Should I buy the stock?"

To each question I offer the same response. "Do you think the stock will go up or down? If you think it's headed up, don't sell it. If you think it will go down, get rid of it."

> **Nobody knows which way the market or any given stock will go.**

The point is, nobody knows which way the market or any given stock will go, least of all me.

As figure 1.3 illustrates, volatility is a consistent part of the market's history. Every investor assumes some risk of loss—and for taking that risk, he or she may get paid a commensurate amount. Of course, the risk taken may, in fact, become an actual cost.

The question each of us must ask is, "How much risk am I willing to accept?" I know a young couple who invested the bulk of their savings in a new company. They had been assured that the stock's value was certain to double, if not triple, within months. For this kind of return the corresponding risk is, of course, tremendous.

Yet so confident were they of success that the couple never seriously considered the risk. "I guess we could lose as much as a third of our investment and still be okay—but really, we won't lose anything," one of them told me. Instead of honestly evaluating the risk, they focused on

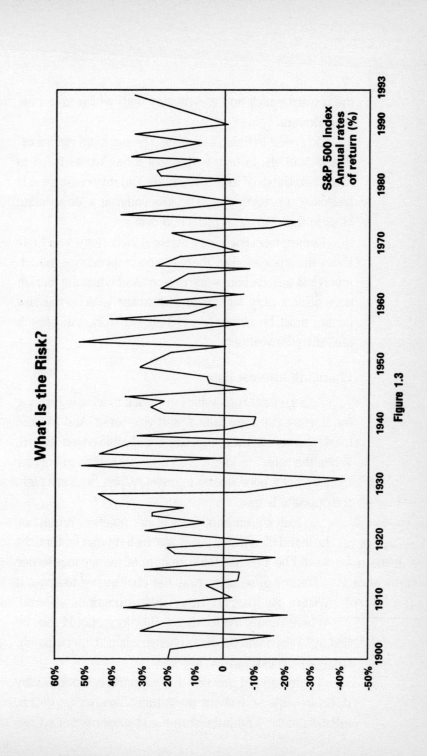

What Is the Risk?

S&P 500 Index
Annual rates
of return (%)

Figure 1.3

the reward: quick and easy money with which to pursue their dreams.

Do I need to finish the story? The stock did not immediately take off; in fact, within just a few weeks it fell to about two-thirds of its original value. Did my young friends feel okay? Certainly not! The loss came as a devastating blow to their financial plans and dreams.

Remember: For every strike-it-rich story you hear about the stock market, there is a corresponding—though much less talked about—tale of woe. And while the market does offer a very legitimate investment vehicle, the risk factors must be carefully weighed. No stock can offer a guaranteed investment.

Changing Interest Rates

As a general rule, when the stock market is heading up, interest rates are falling, and vice versa. And like the market, interest rates represent a double-edged sword. When the rates are low, it is an opportune time to borrow money—but a poor season to invest. When rates are high, the opposite is true.

"Forecasting is very difficult—especially about the future." Judy's grandmother is in her nineties. When her husband died thirty years ago, he left what he thought would be a comfortable amount of money to give her a lifetime of security. Now her challenge is to invest it wisely. As interest rates shift, questions abound. Where should the funds go? How long should they be tied up? When will the rates change again? Unfortunately, there are no easy answers.

There's an old proverb that says, "Forecasting is very difficult—especially about the future." The budget deficit, inflation, taxes, and interest-rate and stock-market swings are just a few of the factors that complicate our planning efforts. Other frightening financial realities include real estate deflation, the declining dollar, and a string of bank and business failures.

Within this uncertain arena, the hope of effective money management seems far-fetched, at best. Is there any way we can achieve financial strength and stability? Must we live at the mercy of circumstances beyond our control?

ARE YOU A THERMOMETER OR A THERMOSTAT?

The economic upheaval caused by problems such as the federal budget deficit and inflation can create a climate of tension, anxiety, and fear. People tend to respond to this environment in one of two ways: Some of us act like thermometers while others behave as thermostats.

Thermometers respond to mounting fear and uncertainty with a jump in their emotional mercury. The red line shoots up, shouting, "Danger! Danger! Rocky road ahead!" Suddenly, even routine tasks can seem impossible, and small obstacles become insurmountable. Fear takes hold, and our strongest instinct is to moan, cry, or collapse in a puddle of ineffectiveness. When the situation stabilizes, our mercury recedes, and we regain a sense of control—at least until the next crisis appears.

Thermometers reflect their environment. Thermostats control their environment.

Often, that crisis is only as far away as the next headline.

Thermometers reflect their environment. They react to and are at the mercy of an ever-changing climate. Thermostats, on the other hand, control their environment.

I have a friend who is a client of our firm. One Christmas when I saw him at a holiday party, he wrapped his arms around me in a giant bear hug and said, with tears in his eyes, "I just want to thank you!"

"For what?" I asked.

"Michigan is in the midst of some really tough economic times," he began, describing a situation I knew to be true. But I wasn't sure why he was thanking me.

In the early eighties my friend had launched his own business. Driven by a fear of failure and the desire to accumulate wealth, he steered the company to remarkable success—borrowing heavily to do so. But as Michigan slid into recession, my friend nearly lost it all. He escaped the collapse—but tumbling real estate prices coupled with escalating interest rates and inflation left him riddled with fear and anxiety about the future.

As he greeted me at the Christmas party, however, he did not look frightened. In fact, he looked happy—yet I knew he was accurate in saying Michigan's economy was struggling.

"I don't know what's ahead," he explained. "Things will probably get worse, but I'm not worried. In fact, I'm actually looking forward to the future!"

I recalled that when my friend had contacted our firm after his initial scare in the early eighties, we had worked with him to develop a plan that would allow him to get out of debt, build liquidity into his financial situation, and significantly increase his charitable giving. Now, like a skilled aerospace engineer awaiting the launch of a newly designed rocket, my friend was eager to witness the strength of his financial strategy under pressure. He had carefully positioned himself in such a way that he would not only *survive* during difficult economic times, he would *thrive*.

My friend is not a one-in-a-million success story. Instead, he represents a financial position that is possible for each of us. We do not have to react to our changing financial climate in a knee-jerk or haphazard fashion. We can become thermostats, controlling our individual environments through proper planning and preparation. We can thrive during economic uncertainty. This should be not merely our *desire*, but our *expectation—* regardless of the financial forecast.

We can thrive during economic uncertainty.

PLANNING FOR A SECURE FUTURE

We have seen how the federal deficit, income taxes, inflation, and the like can sabotage our financial-planning efforts and threaten our personal security. Their impact on the national economy is equally significant. As a result, the desire to harness these problems and manipulate the financial forecast generates more discussion and debate on the floor of the U.S. Congress than anywhere else.

In 1992 I had the opportunity to testify before a Senate subcommittee holding hearings on "Solutions for the New Era: Jobs and Families." While others on the panel pressed for more social programs, I said I believed the American family could benefit from following a four-part financial plan:

1. Spend less than you earn.
2. Avoid the use of debt.
3. Maintain liquidity.
4. Set long-term goals.

The committee chairman listened carefully and re-cited the points back to me. He paused a moment, then said, "It seems like this plan is not just for the family. It seems it would work at any level."

"Yes," I laughed, "including the government!"

I was smiling, but I did not miss the opportunity to exhort the senators to exercise strong leadership through wise financial planning. How, I asked, could they expect the American family not to overspend if the government refuses to provide a proper example of sound money management?

The four principles—living within your income, avoiding debt, staying liquid, and setting goals—are simple.

The four principles—living within your income, avoiding debt, staying liquid, and setting goals—are simple. So simple, in fact, that they may easily be over-looked. Yet they have stood the test of time, having been developed and outlined thousands of years ago in the Old and New Testaments. They are, in fact, the exact same principles our firm relied on to help our clients weather the economic uncertainty in 1982.

Back then, the much-trumpeted survival strategy was to spend and borrow as much as possible as fast as possible because prices and interest rates seemed to know no lim-its. In a deflationary economy, however, just the opposite approach becomes necessary.

As you study today's financial horizon, which will it be: inflation or deflation? Economic growth or a return to recession? Do you know what to expect? Can you guess?

Don Shula, head coach of the Miami Dolphins, re-cently became the "winningest" coach in National Football League history. What is the secret of his success? Most football fans would agree that Shula has benefited from an amazing array of top-notch talent on the field. Early in the 1993 season, however, one sportscaster offered another, more intriguing, assessment.

"Don Shula," he said, "only worries about the things he can control. If something is out of his control, he doesn't give it a second thought."

The wisdom in Shula's strategy may be applied in any arena, from football to finances. We have no individual control over the budget deficit. We cannot influence inflation or guess which way the stock market is going to run. We cannot avoid paying taxes—although in some cases, it's not for any lack of trying!

> **We can control our preparedness to deal with financial realities.**

What we can control is our preparedness to deal with these financial realities. We can, like my friend in Michigan, trade in our thermometer mentality for that of a thermostat. With an effective money-management plan in place, we can approach the future—any future—with a sense of genuine security.

In the coming chapters, you will discover a strategy that takes the guesswork out of financial planning. You will learn to control spending, get out of debt, enjoy liquidity, and set goals for your personal finances. You will confront—and conquer—the most common financial fears. You will find out how to survive—and in fact thrive—regardless of the economic outlook.

> **With an effective money-management plan in place, we can approach the future—any future—with a sense of genuine security.**

Uncertainty is inevitable. Yet by applying the right principles, you can eliminate the possibility of making a wrong or stupid financial move. You need not fear "the system"; in fact, you can let it work entirely to your advantage.

Financial security should be more than just a future hope. It should be your expectation. In the pages ahead, you will learn how to take this expectation and make it a reality in your life!

Dealing with the Fear of Uncertainty

Sherry is a friend of one of my daughters. She had been a missionary, and just before she was to be married, she lived with our family for a few weeks. I will never forget her.

On December 22 Sherry's wedding was only a few months away. As she dashed out to do some last-minute Christmas shopping, she was fairly bursting with her own private joys amid the sparkling holiday season.

All that changed, though, in a matter of minutes. When Sherry returned to the parking lot where she had left her car—in which she kept virtually everything she owned—it was gone. Her car had been stolen. Frantic, she telephoned her fiancé.

"I've got some bad news of my own," came his reply. "I just lost my job."

I would be willing to bet that on that frosty December evening Sherry and her fiancé did not spend their time agonizing over the federal budget deficit or inflation. At that point, they could not have cared less about the tax code or our trade imbalance with Japan. There is something about genuine, personal fear and anxiety that casts a whole new light on the far-off problems that make for national news.

We have all wrestled with our own private worries. In the first chapter we examined the impact of large-scale economic concerns. Now, I want to shift the focus to our individual lives, where our personal fears, desires, and long-range dreams often create an anxiety that far outweighs anything we have ever felt over an increase in inflation or a drop in the Dow.

> **Our fears, desires, and dreams are often entirely valid; yet the emotional punch they pack need not be a knockout blow.**

FEARS, DESIRES, AND LONG-RANGE DREAMS

Our fears, desires, and dreams are often entirely valid; yet the emotional punch they pack need not be a knockout blow. In this chapter you will learn to admit to, and identify, the specific concerns that threaten your personal financial security. Moreover, you will gain a perspective on your financial future that will become the foundation for your ultimate money-management program.

Fears: The Unknown, Unexpected, and Uncertain

A few years ago I knew a family who seemed to have everything. They lived in a nice section of Atlanta and had been blessed with five healthy and active children. The father, a man in his early forties, loved spending time with his kids, and he often took them on special outings.

One weekend he took the older children hiking in the North Carolina mountains. Climbing up a seemingly safe path beside a waterfall, he grabbed a tree branch. The branch broke, and the man plummeted to his death on a rocky ledge below.

How was his wife to cope with rearing five children on her own? In addition to the emotional loss, her financial concerns must have seemed staggering. Could she count on her family and friends? Some—but her husband's business partner was another matter. He sued to get a bigger share of the estate. How do you prepare for something like that?

A prominent businessman from a well-known Boston family recently took his wife and their two children on an annual vacation. Arriving home from the airport, he asked the taxi driver to wait a moment after the family unloaded their belongings. "I'm not staying here," the businessman announced. "I'm filing for divorce. I'm just going inside to get my clothes."

Imagine the family's mental and emotional devastation! And then the fear set in: What would this mean financially? Could the wife rely on her ex-husband's support? Would she and the kids have to move? Would she need to find a job to keep the household going?

A friend of our family recently learned that he has an inoperable brain tumor. He is in his fifties. How will his family respond? Is there ever a way to really be ready to handle the pain and uncertainty of a major illness?

Death, divorce, and unexpected illness all evoke very real and legitimate fears—especially in that they involve factors we typically have little or no control over. Other anxieties include the loss of a job, sudden financial needs (for car repairs or medical expenses, for example), taxes, college costs, and the prospect of retirement living on a fixed income. Even the impending arrival of a new baby—

normally viewed through a window of joyful anticipation—can cause tremendous worry and stress.

Desires: The Goals We Yearn to Achieve

Many of our dreams—in fact, the American dream itself—seem to be vanishing into an early-morning fog.

Our desires may not pack the unplanned-for punch of many of our fears—yet, as causes for anxiety, they are every bit as real. Desires include things like getting out of debt, taking a vacation, buying a home, purchasing clothes, getting a new car, or providing for a child's education in private or Christian schools and continuing through college. The fear that we may fail to realize these goals can exact a devastating emotional toll.

Many of our dreams—in fact, the American dream itself—seem to be vanishing into an early-morning fog. So many of the things we once took for granted are suddenly out of reach. Is it still reasonable to hope, as our parents did, that at some point we may no longer have a home mortgage? Owning our own home used to be considered almost a right; now it seems more like a privilege.

Suddenly, putting your children—or yourself—through college is no longer something to be taken for granted.

The same may be said of a college education. According to the U.S. Department of Education, twenty years ago the annual cost of tuition, room, and board at a four-year public university totaled $1,707. Today, the identical education runs upward of $6,000 per year. Even more daunting is the private-university scenario, where the price tag jumped from $3,512 per year in 1972–1973 to more than $18,000 per year in just two decades! And the skyrocketing costs show no sign of slowing. Suddenly, putting your children—or yourself—through college is no longer something to be taken for granted.

Long-Range Dreams: More Distant Now Than Ever Before?

Further off, but no less vivid, are the hopes and dreams that make for long-term planning. This category may include a desire to launch your own business, increase your charitable giving, or gain the financial independence necessary for retirement.

As we saw in Chapter 1, factors such as tax-code and interest-rate changes make long-range planning especially difficult. Investment counselors urge their clients to get serious about planning—yet they freely admit the challenge this admonition presents. As a T. Rowe Price retirement kit warns, "Planning for retirement is like trying to hit a moving target blindfolded."

So what are we to do? Throw in the investment towel and simply cross our fingers? Start buying lottery tickets in bulk? Hope that rich Uncle Frank will go before we do—and pray that we will get at least some of the inheritance?

> "**P**lanning for retirement is like trying to hit a moving target blindfolded."

I like the way *USA Today*, in a 1993 article on retirement, characterized the typical American attitude: "For many, long-term financial planning has been reduced to simply socking away what they can afford and hoping it all works out. That may be a strategy. But it's no plan."

There is no getting around the fact that we desperately need an effective plan for retirement. Relying on social security alone is not enough; in 1993, the average monthly benefit received by American workers was a meager $629—an income scarcely above the poverty level for people older than sixty-five. And that figure is likely to drop as the social security system adds more and more retirees to its roster—many of whom will live at least ten to twenty years longer than their counterparts of the 1930s and 1940s.

We must confront our fears head-on.

The challenge we face in planning for retirement (or other long-term dreams) can generate a great deal of tension and anxiety. The fear that we might not realize our hopes and desires may prove just as unsettling as the threat of an unexpected loss or crisis. Yet none of these fears should compromise our security. We must confront our fears head-on, wrestling them into submission before they gain a stronghold in our lives.

PINPOINTING YOUR FEARS

It is not sinful or wrong to experience fear, doubt, or uncertainty.

As we have already discussed, there will always be frightening circumstances outside of our control—from the ever-increasing federal deficit to the small, private worries that rob us of our sleep at night. To conquer the negative emotions stirred up by these circumstances, we must first admit to and then specifically identify our fears.

Admit Your Fear

The first step in overcoming financial fear is to face it. It is not sinful or wrong to experience fear, doubt, or uncertainty. Neither is it at all uncommon. Moreover, being a Christian does not make you immune to fear.

Larry Burkett's book *The Coming Economic Earthquake*, which was written primarily for the Christian community, sold about a million copies. Our office received hundreds of phone calls in response to the book—almost all from Christians who were frightened about the economic outlook. Larry never intended that his message be received prophetically; rather, he merely pointed out what would happen if things did not change. He simply made a calculated prediction—yet it was enough to unsettle countless readers!

Fear is a universal emotion. If you doubt me on this, simply open any newspaper and glance through the headlines. The world is glutted with fearful analysts, worried politicians, anxious officials, and countless individuals who are scared about all sorts of things—especially about the future!

We cannot hide our heads in the sand. Refusing to see or acknowledge our fear will not make it go away; in fact, left to fester on its own, it will probably grow to new and more frightening proportions. We must admit that we are afraid—and then move on to tackle our fear.

People wrestle with two primary fears: the fear of failure and the fear of the future.

Identify Your Fear

The second vital step in conquering fear is to identify it. Once you come to grips with the fact that you are experiencing fear (once you admit it, that is), you must label your specific concerns. A correct diagnosis of the problem is essential to discovering the proper cure.

As a financial counselor, I have found that people wrestle with two primary fears: the fear of failure and the fear of the future. I think psychologists would equate the fear of failure with our search for *significance*, while the fear of the future represents our search for *security*. In terms of financial planning, our thinking often runs along these lines: "If I have enough wealth, I will be secure (or significant or both)."

1. **The Fear of Failure.** I grew up amid modest surroundings; we were neither poor nor rich. Neither of my parents graduated from college, but as a factory foreman, my father provided for our family's needs. Even so, I remember envying my schoolmates who seemed to be able to purchase new clothes at will or who had their own cars at age sixteen.

As a teenager, I stepped from an eighth-grade class of only twelve students into a high school where there were six hundred students in my class alone. I desperately wanted to be "someone," and by the time I graduated, I had lettered in two sports, served as senior-class president, and achieved the distinction I craved.

I continued to make a name for myself in college and then went on to pass the CPA exam on my first try. Later I acquired my MBA degree and got a job with the world's largest accounting firm.

To an outside observer, my life appeared to be woven with the threads of success. I typically worked seventy- to eighty-hour weeks, relying on my accumulating wealth to give me a feeling of significance and success. What I did not realize, however, was that a fear of failure dictated my every move.

Once I committed my life to Christ, nothing changed. I still worked more than seventy hours a week, this time for the "cause of Christ." I thrived on the recognition I received from the Christian community, and my reputation as a hardworking, dedicated Christian brought me immense satisfaction. It reached the point where, in my mind, it seemed that the church—if not the Lord Himself—were somehow dependent on my outstanding efforts.

Finally, a friend pointed out that, as a Christian, I was

allowing myself to be driven by the very same force that had influenced my lifestyle in the secular world. The fear of failure was just as wrong in the one arena as in the other, with consequences that were no less adverse.

The fear of failure—or in other words, the search for significance—is typically more of a male issue than a female one. Men, more often than women, tend to be driven by the fear that if they do not push hard enough or work long enough, they will fail. Often, this drive can have positive results in terms of increased productivity and greater financial reward; such was the case with my Michigan friend described in Chapter 1. As he was, many successful entrepreneurs and business executives are propelled—sometimes unknowingly—by the fear of failure.

The danger, however, is that when money and possessions become our preeminent measures of success and significance, anything that threatens our ability to accumulate wealth becomes a driving force in our decision-making process. Ultimately, this mind-set leads to unwise decisions and wrong financial moves.

Many successful entrepreneurs and business executives are propelled— sometimes unknowingly— by the fear of failure.

Once I recognized how common—and powerful— the fear of failure was, I began to recognize its presence in my decision making. When I launched my present company, I was determined not to allow my own fear—and my own need for significance—to establish a foothold. I refused to continue my workaholic lifestyle, and I set an example that let my employees know they were not expected to work long hours at night or on weekends.

Our staff works about forty to fifty hours per week— an average markedly less than the norm in most professional and executive offices. Interestingly enough, our business continues to grow by 15 to 20 percent each year. I believe this increase is due to God's gracious provision. Once I removed my own fear of failure from the situation, the Lord was free to guide and direct us according to His schedule rather than mine.

We must face the fear of failure, not only on the financial level, but also on a spiritual level. If you are a Christian, you have already dealt with this issue. You are already an admitted failure! You have recognized that you can do nothing to save yourself or to earn your own significance.

Jesus Christ is the only true source of personal worth and fulfillment. As 2 Corinthians 3:5 reminds us, we are not "sufficient," or competent, to claim anything for ourselves, "but our sufficiency is from God." Once we truly believe this promise, the fear of failure—and its accompanying desires for material or worldly significance—will no longer dictate our decisions and behavior.

> **We must face the fear of failure, not only on the financial level, but also on the spiritual level.**

2. The Fear of the Future. My mother was a tremendous worrier. She seemed to feel that if she worried enough she could somehow manipulate the future. And ultimately that is what worry is all about: *Worry is an attempt to control the future.*

All of us worry to some extent. A sage once said 98 percent of what we worry about never comes to pass—proving, of course, that worry really does work!

> **Worry is an attempt to control the future.**

Worry is a common manifestation of the fear of the future. The things we worry about—such as the death of a spouse, a medical emergency, unrealized dreams, or a financial calamity—are the things that affect our sense of security. Because we can readily point to these concerns, the fear of the future is usually much easier to identify than the fear of failure.

Again, identifying this fear is half the battle. Once we recognize that we are afraid of the future, we can pinpoint the exact problem and develop an effective solution. As with the fear of failure, we must evaluate the fear of the future on two levels, the spiritual and the financial.

Scripture is loaded with truth and wisdom about the future and how we are to approach it. In Luke 14:28 Jesus asks, "Which of you, intending to build a tower, does not sit down first and count the cost, whether he has enough to finish it?" Obviously, there is wisdom in accurate financial planning for the future.

At the same time, though, the Bible warns us that we cannot control the future. James 4:14 reminds us that we "do not know what will happen tomorrow. For what is your life? It is even a vapor that appears for a little time and then vanishes away."

One of my favorite passages about the future and the time we have is 2 Peter 3:8: "With the Lord one day is as a thousand years, and a thousand years as one day."

When I last spoke with Joni Eareckson Tada, she shared her thoughts on this verse. Paralyzed after a diving accident, Joni is a popular author, speaker, and entertainer who has a dynamic ministry to the disabled. I had always interpreted 2 Peter 3:8 to mean that since a day was like a thousand years, God was not anxious about schedules or timetables. After all, He has all the time in the world! While I still believe this assessment to be true, Joni opened my eyes to the other side of the verse. Since a thousand years is like a day, Joni said, each day becomes incredibly important in that it can have the eternal impact of a thousand years!

The spiritual principles outlined in 2 Peter 3:8 are also appropriate on a financial level. The knowledge that time is not as short as it may appear to be will keep us from plunging headlong into an ill-considered plan or investment. On the other hand, the realization of each day's potential can motivate us to action where we might otherwise drag our feet. Either way, the smartest approach to any financial decision begins with confronting your concerns.

> **The smartest approach to any financial decision begins with confronting your concerns.**

Face Your Fear

Nobody is immune to fear. Chances are, your personal concerns and private worries will fit into at least one, if not both, of the two fear categories we have discussed: the fear of failure and the fear of the future. Have you admitted there are areas of your financial life that cause you to be afraid? What are they?

Take a few moments to mentally catalog your financial fears. Do any of the following items threaten your sense of security? Review this list, marking any areas that reflect your individual concerns.

____ A. Past mistakes
- Financially, if you could do one thing over, what would it be?

_____

_____

- Are there other financial mistakes you have made that are creating anxiety right now?

_____

_____

_____ B. Future dreams, desires, goals, opportunities
     _____ Children's education
     _____ Personal education
     _____ Retirement
     _____ Financial independence
     _____ Starting your own business
     _____ Purchasing first or new home
     _____ Paying off debt
     _____ Other: _____

_____ C. Future uncertainties, challenges, fears
     _____ Death of a loved one causing personal financial hardship
     _____ Loss of a job
     _____ Medical/health/accident-related concerns
     _____ Business failure
     _____ Investment losses
     _____ Other: _____

_____ D. External forces
     _____ The national economy
     _____ Tax-law changes
     _____ Other: _____

Deal with Your Fear

Having pinpointed your specific fears, work through the following steps to deal with your concerns. (Hint: If you cannot confidently answer all the questions in this section, come back and complete this page when you finish reading this book.)

A. Of all the fears you identified and checked, cross off those that are out of your control.

B. Of those that are left, identify your top two fears:
    1. _____
    2. _____

C. How likely is it that number 1 will occur? _____ percent chance
    How likely is it that number 2 will occur? _____ percent chance

D. If number 1 does occur, what is the financial cost? $_____
    If number 2 does occur, what is the financial cost? $_____

E. What are the steps you can take to prepare for number 1?

1. _____
2. _____
3. _____
4. _____
5. _____

What are the steps you can take to prepare for number 2?

1. _____
2. _____
3. _____
4. _____
5. _____

Put Your Fear into Perspective

As we discovered in the lesson from 2 Peter 3:8, understanding and applying God's perspective on time steals much of the thunder from our fears about the future. Likewise, putting our concerns into the proper perspective goes a long way toward rendering our fears powerless to dictate or influence our decision making.

The Bible relates story after story of the fears and concerns that stalked God's people. Joseph, Gideon, and Paul were as flawed and human as any of us—yet in their stories we can find great encouragement and a host of "how-to's" for putting fear into perspective.

A. Read Genesis 41. How did Joseph deal with the fear of famine?

_____
_____
_____

B. Read Judges 6 and 7. How did Gideon deal with the fear of a powerful enemy?

_____
_____
_____

C. Read Acts 16:16–40. How did Paul deal with being suddenly thrown into prison?

_____

_____

_____

D. Meditate on Philippians 4:6–7 and 1 Thessalonians 5:18. Have you brought every fear to God, as He commands? Will you resolve to do so?

Admitting and identifying your specific concerns is the first step in dealing with the fear of uncertainty. Even then, though, such fear can worm its way into your financial life and create panic—or, equally devastating, leave you paralyzed and unable to take decisive action.

In the next chapter we will explore the consequences of your financial concerns. As we do, you will learn to fortify yourself in a position of uncompromised freedom from fear—even amid the most uncertain or unstable financial conditions. Armed with such a proactive approach to financial planning, you can maximize your potential for prosperity and look forward to a secure and stable future.

3

Be Proactive

**Stocks Plummet
Amid Panicky Selling**

On October 20, 1987, the *Wall Street Journal*—and every other newspaper in the nation—trumpeted the news of the stock market's biggest-ever one-day plunge. As the bears ran wild on Wall Street, investors began to talk in terms of Doomsday. Could it be the Great Depression all over again?

The crash of October 1929—"Black Tuesday"—heralded stock-market losses that, within two months, totaled forty billion dollars—exceeding the entire cost to the United States of World War I! More than five thousand bank failures followed; people lost their homes and farms to foreclosure, and joblessness became the plague of the nation.

When the news of the 1987 crash hit, our firm was already advising about five hundred clients on money management. As investors considered their holdings on that gloomy October morning after the unprecedented plunge, the fantastic losses of 1929 loomed large. Our office was swamped with phone calls. Each caller wondered if it was time to sell in a scramble to "save-what-may." Each asked the identical question: "What should I do?"

Unexpected events such as the 1987 market crash bring our worst nightmares to life. The question of what to do in a crisis situation is a universal concern. Many people panic, others are paralyzed by fear, and still others fall prey to the temptations that uncertainty creates.

In this chapter we will unmask the twin threats of panic and paralysis. We will also disarm fear's ability to lure us toward improper and unwise financial footings. Then, by accepting responsibility for the future, you will learn to take a proactive approach to financial management and discover the secret to true prosperity.

The fact that the October 1987 fall was so dramatic did not seem, in itself, to be reason to dismiss an entire financial strategy.

THE PERILS OF PANIC

When the stock market crashed in 1987, the first telephone call I received was from my parents. Never having invested in anything riskier than CDs, they had finally opted to buy into some no-load mutual funds in August of 1987—when, in retrospect, the market peaked. Like the other callers, they wanted to know whether they should sell.

I gave my parents the same advice we gave all our clients: "Do not do anything." Although we had no idea what the future held, we recognized that our clients' financial plans had been laid with an eye toward the long term. We knew to expect ups and downs; the fact that the October fall was so dramatic did not seem, in itself, to be reason to dismiss an entire financial strategy.

The good news is that my parents did not risk all their savings in mutual funds. The bad news is that as first-time investors they allowed fear to dictate their decisions. Afraid to hang on and weather the storm, they sold the bulk of their holdings in December—when the market finally bottomed out.

Of course, nobody could have predicted that by January of 1988 the market would recover almost 100 percent and that within five years the Dow-Jones Industrial Average would double, from seventeen hundred to a then-unbelievable thirty-four hundred.

Without the benefit of such foreknowledge, many investors viewed the 1987 crash from a perspective of panic. One of our five hundred clients terminated his relationship with our firm, pulling all of his money out of the market in a fear-driven frenzy. I heard a similar story about another client who had left our firm a few months before the crash. We had not been "aggressive" enough to suit him, he said. He had wanted to invest most of his life savings entirely in the stock market, which seemed—to him—to know no limits. When he left us, he bought the most aggressive stocks he could find. On October 20, the day after the crash, he panicked and sold everything—at just about the worst possible time.

Sources of Panic

Panic often stems from two sources: the fear of a missed opportunity and the fear of an economic or political collapse.

1. **Fear of a Missed Opportunity.** In the 1970s and early 1980s when inflation ran rampant, it seemed that everyone wanted to invest in gold and silver. The price of gold set new records almost daily, and in a time of cheapening dollars and a failing economy, precious metals appeared to be a safe and lucrative haven. Fear and greed combined to turn gold and silver into a seemingly "unbeatable" investment opportunity.

One of our clients became so caught up in the fear and greed frenzy that he bought twenty thousand dollars' worth of silver. I remember the difficulty we had as our staff tried to lug the purchase to his car—he had acquired so much silver he could not even carry it!

Who could have guessed that, within a year or two, gold and silver would represent the worst possible investment? Their skyward trend faltered and then fell, and investors who made rushed (and late) decisions to protect themselves with precious metals after 1982 or 1983 got badly burned.

> **Surefire "opportunities of a lifetime" arise every day, from business deals to stock-market "finds."**

Surefire "opportunities of a lifetime" arise every day, from business deals to stock-market "finds." I view these investments with a skeptical eye, keeping in mind three rules: First, if it sounds too good to be true, it probably is. Second, there are no "bad deals." And finally, I have lived long enough to know that there is always another "guaranteed opportunity" coming tomorrow.

In addition to the fear of a missed opportunity, panic may result from the fear of an external force we have no control over, such as an economic or political collapse.

2. **Fear of Forces Beyond Our Control.** Our firm had a client named Bill, the head of a large corporation,

who asked us to manage his company's pension fund. He had benefited from the personal financial plan he had established with our help, and he was eager to develop a similar program for his employees.

You can imagine my surprise when I learned that a week after Bill solicited our help on the pension fund he wanted to take all of his personal holdings out of the stock market and convert everything to cash. Curious about his sudden change of heart, I discovered he had just taken a trip to the West Coast. There, several archconservative economic analysts had convinced him of an impending financial collapse in which the entire nation would become bankrupt. Terrified by that prospect, Bill panicked, grabbed his money, and ran.

How can you tell if a decision is motivated by fear or simply by conservative caution? A "gloom-and-doom" forecast may be entirely legitimate, yet it should never be the foundation of your decision making.

Fear-based decisions may be characterized by one or more of the following traits:

> **A "gloom-and-doom" forecast may be entirely legitimate, yet it should never be the foundation of your decision making.**

- The decision is made quickly, with little forethought.
- The decision is presumptive, based on conclusions that have little or no substantiating proof.
- The decision is ill-advised, having been made under the counsel of untested, unreliable, or biased sources.

A fear-based decision often has an accompanying gut reaction of anxiety or tension. By contrast, wise and thoughtful decisions are usually characterized by a sense of stability and calm. Scripture attests to this pattern. Philippians 4:7 promises that, "the peace of God, which surpasses all understanding, will guard your hearts and minds through Christ Jesus." Good decisions, financial and otherwise, are marked by peace, not panic.

THE PARALYSIS PROBLEM

> Good decisions, financial and otherwise, are marked by peace, not panic.

Panic can ruin even the best-laid financial plans. Equally devastating, though, is an inability to act. Fear of making a wrong decision can result in our making no decision at all. Or we may get caught in "analysis paralysis," endlessly weighing our options until we are completely unable to make a move of any kind.

> Fear of making a wrong decision can result in our making no decision at all.

Nancy was in her early thirties when she came to our firm for financial advice. Her husband had been killed in a car accident, and she had received more than a million dollars in the insurance settlement. Concerned about her ability to provide for her young children, Nancy had contacted my friend and fellow author, Larry Burkett. Because Larry's ministry does not do investment counseling, he referred her to us.

We met with Nancy several times with the goal of helping her invest the money to provide long-term security for her family. At the time, money-market accounts offered an incredible 18 percent return—yet Nancy never felt able to make even that low-risk investment. So frightened was she of making a wrong move that she simply kept the million dollars in her checkbook! The good news was that a million dollars is a million dollars, no matter where it sits. The bad news for Nancy is that she allowed

fear to paralyze her and rob her of the tremendous potential she possessed.

As you consider any financial decision, three simple
questions are useful in gauging your degree of panic,
paralysis, or peace:

- What is the very worst that can happen if I do (or
  do not do) this?
- How likely is that worst-case scenario to occur?
- Am I willing to live with the consequences—favor-
  able or not—of this decision?

The answers to these questions will help remove the
biases created by fear and greed, allow you to view your
options objectively, and help you honestly evaluate your
level of peace.

TACKLING TEMPTATION

One prevalent notion adding fuel to the fires of
panic and paralysis is that we live in the absolute worst
time in history in terms of the sinfulness of our generation. "How will we survive?" we wonder. "Does God
realize what's going on? Isn't He worried?"

> Christians throughout the ages have wrestled with identical questions.

The truth is, Christians throughout the ages have
wrestled with identical questions. Ancient Roman believ-
ers, medieval monks, and even our Puritan ancestors must
have looked in dismay at the world around them and ques-
tioned whether God was sleeping, or perhaps on vacation.

Today, rather than allowing the spiritual and economic fragility of our society to corner us with fear and

uncertainty, we must go on the offensive. Christ knew the trials His disciples—and we—would face, and He provided a battle plan: "Watch and pray," He said, "lest you enter into temptation" (Mark 14:38).

Probably the single greatest temptation during times of economic uncertainty is to hoard our wealth. This desire is nothing new. In Luke 12 Christ told of a rich fool who thought he could protect himself by building bigger barns to store his better-than-expected crops. Having thus secured his economic future, the fellow reasoned he could "eat, drink, and be merry" (v. 19), enjoying his good fortune on easy street.

This story illustrates three temptations fear and uncertainty can create:

> **Probably the single greatest temptation during times of economic uncertainty is to hoard our wealth.**

The first temptation is a longing for a life of comfort and ease. The rich fool probably figured he had worked hard managing his farm and that he deserved to enjoy his remaining years in comfort. Likewise, most Americans look forward to their retirement years. The thought that some financial calamity could prevent their "rightful relaxation" is intolerable.

To me, however, the resort communities and fun-in-the-sun spots that dot our southern and coastal landscapes are the most depressing places in the world! I do not condemn retirement; on the contrary, our firm helps people plan to enjoy it. I do, however, feel very strongly that a life of leisure and total freedom from responsibility has no place in a God-directed plan. Christians should never retire. They may leave their paying jobs or change vocations, but their newfound freedom should not be used exclusively for self-indulgence and enter-

> **Christians should never retire.**

tainment. Instead, it should become a vehicle for fulfilling God's call to service.

The second temptation is the perceived right to a particular lifestyle. Just as the rich fool wanted to "eat, drink, and be merry," we have all sorts of similar desires and demands.

The ten-year-old boy must have the right pair of athletic shoes—despite a price tag topping one hundred dollars. By the time that same boy turns sixteen, he will expect a car—and not just any old jalopy. Next, it's a college education and then a particular job.

I remember a television advertisement for a certain investment and financial-planning firm. It featured an airline pilot whose job was to fly the daily shuttle from Newark to Chicago. Then the scene switched to a picturesque island setting in which a prop plane skimmed the crystal, turquoise water and flew off into the sunset.

The message was clear: Condemned to travel the same old flight path day in and day out, the pilot's life reeked of boredom and insignificance. Had he contacted the investment firm to better manage his resources, he could have chucked that awful job and launched his own freewheeling, glamorous, island-hopping air service where the sparkling beaches and sunny, blue skies promised a life of total luxury and fulfillment.

"What's wrong," I exploded, "with being a commercial pilot?" To me, being able to fly anything—from a glider to a space shuttle—is a glamorous job. And with the airline industry downsizing virtually across the board, I can think of several out-of-work pilots who—glamorous or not—certainly see their former job as one they wish they could have kept.

The list goes on and on. After we land that perfect job, we want a lovely house in a good neighborhood. Then it's the right vacation, followed by the acquisition of a second home, and ultimately, retirement.

When we view things as our "rights," any threat to our achieving them becomes intolerable.

When we view these things as our "rights," any threat to our achieving them becomes intolerable. The thought of not getting into a "good" college or being able to afford that ski-lodge getaway fills us with great anxiety and fear. Yet none of these things that make for a "desirable" lifestyle are our inalienable rights. We must watch out for this kind of desire and pray against that temptation.

Nowhere does the Bible give any indication that we can do anything to protect or save ourselves.

The third temptation is the desire to protect ourselves from the consequences of economic uncertainty. The rich fool wanted to build bigger barns to create self-sufficiency in his financial future. Yet this kind of protection is not our responsibility. It is God's.

God promises to protect us. Psalm 50:14–15 paints God as our source of help:

Offer to God thanksgiving,
And pay your vows to the Most High.
Call upon Me in the day of trouble;
I will deliver you, and you shall glorify Me.

Inherent in these verses is the need to credit God with our protection and deliverance. Nowhere does the

Bible give any indication that we can do anything to protect or save ourselves.

God does, however, vest us with the responsibility to provide for our families. Proverbs 6:6–8 advises us to consider the hardworking ant, that "Provides her supplies in the summer, / And gathers her food in the harvest." Moreover, God's view of those who fail to provide is clear in 1 Timothy 5:8: "If anyone does not provide for his own, and especially for those of his household, he has denied the faith and is worse than an unbeliever."

Thus, being able to provide for your family becomes a legitimate concern. Many Christians, however, take this responsibility to an extreme, allowing their responsibility for provision to become a self-sufficient desire to protect. A hoarding mentality ensues, driving people to "build bigger barns" as a hedge against an uncertain future.

There was a used-car salesman named Ned that I know who qualified as a modern-day "bigger-barn builder." He never went to college, and never had very much money. In the late sixties, however, he managed to purchase a quick-print franchise. Business took off, and he quickly franchised several more shops.

Ned's income jumped from next to nothing to more than a million dollars per year. He moved to Florida, bought a yacht, and prepared to enjoy a life free from need and want.

At age forty-five, Ned had a heart attack. His life of ease and luxury instantly disappeared. In its place arose an existence dictated by a restricted diet and regimented exercise. I have often thought about Ned and wondered to myself, "What good did it really do him to accumulate all that wealth?"

Many of us sense that, if we can just save X amount of money or purchase Y amount of stocks, bonds, and life insurance, we will somehow be okay. Like Ned, we think—foolishly—that we can do a better job than God when it comes to protecting ourselves.

Our protection is God's job—and yet we must recognize our own accountability for good stewardship. My wife, Judy, and I like to remind each other, "You can only do what you can do, and only you can do what you can do." Your talents and abilities are unique; the circumstances of your life are yours alone to confront.

So what can you do? In financially difficult times, you can confront uncertainty from a perspective of peace instead of panic or paralysis. You can, as Christ commands, "watch and pray" against the temptation to hoard your resources in a futile attempt to protect yourself. Trusting in God's guidance, you can establish plans, make decisions, and accept responsibility for your own actions.

You can only do what you can do, and only you can do what you can do.

THE PROACTIVE APPROACH TO PROSPERITY

Stephen Covey, in his phenomenally successful book *Seven Habits of Highly Effective People*, explained what it means to be proactive. Covey's habit number 1 states, "You are responsible for your life. Decide what you should do and get on with it." Long before Covey's book hit the stands, a proactive approach to financial planning typically spelled the difference between direction and disaster.

My firm has a client on the East Coast, Jerry, who got into the real estate business in the late sixties and became very successful. In 1985, he decided to quit. Having made plenty of money, he said to himself, "Enough is enough." With that, he converted his business assets into other investments—and subsequently upped his annual giving to the six-figure level.

Jerry's move drew questions and criticism from many of his friends and business associates. Why, people wondered, would anyone with such an apparent "Midas touch" decide to leave it all behind? Jerry had been the epitome of success—how could he simply end it all?

Jerry never was one to sit around and wait for things to happen. He took control of his situation and made his own moves. His exit was, in fact, part of a long-term plan. And in retrospect, Jerry's critics had to concede that he had made the right move—especially since the real estate market tumbled dramatically shortly after he left and he was later able to buy up many of his former holdings at substantially reduced prices!

Proactivity is a strategy that works at any income level.

I know what you are thinking. You think Jerry was able to leave his job because he was rich. "Sure," you are saying to yourself, "I'd quit too—if I had a cool couple of million to do it with."

You may be missing the point. Jerry was able to walk away, not because of his wealth, but because he had taken control of his resources and established a workable plan. He was proactive—a strategy that works at any income level.

For example: Joan was a single young professional who earned a good income working for a major corporation. Even so, she never seemed to have any money to spare. Saddled with a stack of credit-card bills and car payments, she felt she could never get ahead.

Then Joan read my book *Master Your Money.* She developed a budget and began to take control of her spending. Within just two or three years, she had worked herself into a strong financial position that included savings, no debt, and a controlled lifestyle.

Just about the only thing wrong with Joan's picture was her job. She was not happy because her work environment clashed with her personal value system. Thanks to her strong, proactive planning, Joan was able to leave her job. With a secure financial foundation, she took a year to carefully select another position—which, happily for us, was with our firm.

In her disciplined approach to financial planning, Joan reminds me of Judy's Aunt Avis. Aunt Avis never married. She never got a driver's license, and she held only one job. She was a schoolteacher from the moment she finished college until her retirement at age sixty-five.

Aunt Avis epitomized responsible planning and proactive money management. She lived nearly a quarter-century in retirement, during which she continued her wise financial stewardship. She lived within her income from social security and her teacher's retirement plan— rarely, if ever, dipping into her life savings. Having paid off her mortgage years earlier, she continued to avoid the use of debt.

Thanks to this careful money management, Aunt Avis enjoyed her retirement. A broken furnace, medical bills, and other unexpected mishaps posed no threat because she had already set aside ample funds to meet such needs. Never once did Aunt Avis experience financial fear—even though, during her retirement, the stock market crashed twice and interest rates varied from 3 to 22 percent!

Neither Joan nor Aunt Avis could be described as being very wealthy, yet neither allowed herself to be controlled or victimized by her circumstances. Like Jerry, the women refused to become trapped. Criticism from business associates, the lure of more and more money, the mire of an unfulfilling job, and the uncertainty of retirement living were no match for the proactive lifestyles adopted by these three wise individuals.

Thinking proactively also helps lift the confusion from the decision-making process that surrounds financial planning. Judy and I recently talked with Tom and Susan, a young couple who had been married for just over a year. Enticed by low interest rates and frightened by the prospect of "throwing money away" on rent, they were eager to get our advice on buying a home.

> **Don't confuse an economic decision with one that simply has economic consequences.**

As we talked, it became apparent that Susan, especially, wanted the security and comfort of a family "nest." I could understand that—but before I could give them a green light on the housing purchase, I needed to ask a few questions.

"How long do you plan to stay in your present job?" I asked. "Do you want to have children? Is Atlanta where you would like to live five or ten years from now? Are you satisfied in your church home?"

These were the kinds of questions that needed answers before Tom and Susan could take the mortgage plunge. The couple's problem was a common one: They had confused an economic decision with one that simply had economic consequences.

Buying a house is not an economic decision. Of course, accepting a mortgage has economic consequences, but acquiring a home itself should be part of an overall, proactive plan. Rather than asking, "Should we buy a house now while interest rates are low?" (a question that boxes the home buyer into a strictly economic mind-set), Tom and Susan needed to take responsibility for their future. Instead of wondering about a home purchase, they needed to ask, "What do we want to be when we grow up?" By correctly defining the objective, they could take the proper proactive steps toward achieving their ultimate goal.

And Peace Will Follow

My firm is in the business of imparting peace of mind to people who want to take proactive and responsible control of their resources. Jerry, Joan, and Aunt Avis all enjoyed peace of mind—thanks to their proactive choices. They did not fear a job loss, a new tax law, or any other unexpected threat. Consequently, they were able to realize both their desires as well as their long-range dreams.

Peace of mind, as you will discover in this book, is the foundation of prosperity.

Peace of mind, as you will discover in this book, is the foundation of prosperity. Scripture is full of admonitions against fearfulness. Hand in hand with these verses are promises of God's provision. He is fully aware of our fears and desires—as Matthew 6:8 says, "Your Father knows the things you have need of before you ask Him."

God will provide. He has already given us a scriptural outline for proactive financial planning. The points are the same ones I detailed in Chapter 1, when I told you about my speaking before the congressional subcommittee, and they are the same ones Aunt Avis relied on to secure her financial future: Spend less than you earn, avoid debt, maintain liquidity, and establish long-term goals.

Obviously, this approach is more complicated than it sounds. In Parts 2 and 3 of this book we will walk through the eight tried-and-true steps that put this approach into action. By creating—and practicing—your own proactive plan, you will defeat fear and uncertainty and enjoy a thriving financial future.

PART
TWO

PREPARING YOUR PERSONAL STORM SHELTER

Step 1:
Take a
Financial
Physical

Joseph is one of my heroes. Sold into slavery by his jealous brothers, propositioned and then slandered by his boss's wife, and finally thrown into prison where he was forgotten for years, Joseph remained faithful to God. Even the lure of sudden fame and prosperity failed to tempt his eyes away from the Lord.

My spirit is attracted to Joseph's faithfulness. My mind, however, is impressed by something else. As an accountant and financial adviser, I find Joseph's ability to handle resources and plan for the future particularly appealing. He had no academic or vocational training, yet thanks to his foresight and effective planning, he was able to thrive during a worldwide economic catastrophe.

Joseph's story, detailed in Genesis 39 through 41, offers valuable lessons for contemporary financial planning. We're told Joseph was "handsome in form and appearance" (39:6). When he resisted the sexual advances of his master's wife, she turned the tables and had him thrown into prison on trumped-up charges of attempted rape.

During his imprisonment Joseph developed a reputation as an interpreter of dreams. When this talent came to Pharaoh's attention, he called on Joseph to explain two disturbing dreams. After listening to Pharaoh's account of the visions, Joseph revealed their meaning: Egypt was destined for seven years of agricultural abundance, followed by seven years of severe famine. Joseph then recommended a plan for storing food during the good years so the nation could survive the lean. Pharaoh liked the suggestion. Even more, he liked Joseph—and he immediately placed the handsome, young Hebrew in charge of all Egypt.

A PROACTIVE PLAN: LESSONS FROM JOSEPH

Joseph began his tenure as Egypt's CEO by touring the country to assess the state of the nation. At the time, the harvests were plentiful. I imagine Joseph surveyed the territory, noted population levels and needs, and monitored crops and grain production.

Next, he established a goal. Simply put, Joseph wanted Egypt to survive the seven years of famine that lay ahead.

Finally, Joseph developed a plan. During the seven years of abundance that preceded the famine, he "gathered very much grain, as the sand of the sea, until he stopped counting, for it was immeasurable" (Gen. 41:49).

Joseph's approach parallels the strategy our firm employs to help clients plan for their own financial future. Like Joseph, we use a three-pronged attack:

1. Take a financial physical. The beginning point of responsible, proactive money management is to determine the actual state of your finances. Most people are simply not realistic about where they are financially—and yet, if a person's physical health were at stake, he or she would certainly be entirely candid with a physician. Just as a doctor needs the proper facts to make a correct diagnosis, a financial physical must also be completely accurate and honest.

2. Establish a finish line. Decide where you want to go, and then develop sound financial goals. Whether you want to provide for a college education, debt reduction, retirement, long-term giving, or something else, you must establish the objectives, discuss them openly with your spouse, write them down, and keep them in prayer.

> **Most people are simply not realistic about where they are financially.**

3. Plan how to get from here to there. An effective plan for getting from point one to point two is actually a five-step process:

a. Learn to live within your income.
b. Get out of debt.
c. Increase your giving.
d. Become your own bank (increase your liquidity).
e. Invest to preserve wealth.

The true test of how well your strategy will work is to see how it holds up in the real world of finances, from the rosiest, best-case outlook to the absolute worst-case scenario.

Paul Zane Pilzer, in his book *Unlimited Wealth,* makes

a compelling case for a future of prosperity. An adviser to the Reagan and Bush administrations and the managing partner of a national real estate investment company, Pilzer says we are entering a period of wealth and productivity unlike anything the world has ever experienced. Information is now being processed so quickly that technological changes beyond our current comprehension become entirely possible.

Pilzer theorizes that "the more we earn, the more we spend; the more we spend, the more we get; the more we get, the more we want; and the more we want, the harder we seem to be willing to work to earn more money to get it." This, he maintains, is the driving force—and the guaranteeing factor—behind prosperity.

By contrast, Harry E. Figgie, Jr., sees no cause for rejoicing in our financial future. A well-respected businessman and the cochairman of President Reagan's Private Sector Survey on Cost Control (popularly known as the Grace Commission), Figgie has written an intriguing book called *Bankruptcy 1995*. His thesis is that our escalating deficit will soon force the country into bankruptcy.

This perspective is shared by many economists who maintain that consumer confidence—which serves as the basis for our currency's value—will continue to be eroded by our monstrous deficit. As a result, they say, hyperinflation will cause an ultimate financial collapse, as it did in Germany's Weimar Republic and in the recent economic situation in Russia.

Another school of thought predicts a coming deflationary depression that will overshadow the Great Depression of the 1930s. Continued business layoffs will mean fewer and fewer buyers, which will, in turn, create a dramatic drop in prices and an eventual giant depression.

Still another gloomy scenario calls for a total political and economic collapse, such as we witnessed in Eastern Europe and the former Soviet Union. The American economy could conceivably get so bad that a dictator or military commander could step in and, with very little opposition, disband the existing power structures as we know them. Never in America? Just ask Russia's hard-line Communists what they once thought about similar prospects in the Soviet Union!

Given these differing scenarios, consider how your financial strategy might work:

If Pilzer is right and we wind up in an era of incredible wealth (the best-case scenario), everybody wins. However, having already worked to get out of debt, you will be in a position to use prosperity to further your advantage. You may continue to retire debt, increase your giving, or make additional wise investments—all of which will bring you that much closer to achieving your ultimate goals.

If, on the other hand, Figgie's prognosis is correct and we head down the road toward hyperinflation, your financial plan will have set you up in a position of security. Thanks to your efforts to retire debt and control spending, you will have more of your own money available to take advantage of inflationary opportunities and investments.

Likewise, during a time of deflation and depression, liquidity often spells the difference between sinking and survival. Your debt-free position will mean that, unlike others, you will not lose your assets. Moreover, having a cash reserve will allow you the freedom to choose from a host of attractive buying opportunities as prices continue to tumble.

And finally, if the worst case should occur and we find ourselves in the midst of an all-out political and economic collapse, you can credit your financial plan with enabling you to be the best possible steward of your resources during a time of supreme uncertainty.

Before we go on, let me quickly point out that I am not saying any of this—from ultimate prosperity to impending collapse—will happen. The Old Testament penalty for false prophecy was death—a consequence I hope to avoid, at least for the next few decades! I am not prophesying, I am not predicting, I am not even hazarding a guess about the future.

> **You need to take a financial physical.**

Instead, I am simply trying to help you plot a winning financial strategy, one that will work no matter what the future holds. And the first step is to accurately assess your personal financial circumstances. You need to take a financial physical.

GETTING STARTED: THE FINANCIAL PHYSICAL

As with any new discipline or plan, getting started is always the hardest part. When I turned forty I began to worry about my health for the first time. I decided to assess the situation with a first-rate, all-encompassing, no-secrets-allowed physical at the Cooper Clinic in Dallas. In short, it was not a pleasant experience.

Starved after not being allowed to eat for twenty-four hours before the tests, I spent the entire day decked out in one of those tie-in-the-back hospital gowns. I was cold, embarrassed, humiliated, and worst of all, terrified of what the results might be.

That was then. Looking back, it really was not that bad, and my sense of relief at learning that I was okay more than made up for any previous discomfort. Likewise, a financial physical is almost never pleasant. At the very least, it may be tedious or time consuming—yet just knowing where you are will come as a refreshing comfort. Even if the results of your financial physical indicate a need for some immediate "surgery," you can feel assured that simply taking the physical will put you well on your way to a healthier financial performance.

A financial physical is almost never pleasant.

The Critical Questions

A financial physical involves answering four significant questions:

1. What do I owe?
2. What do I own?
3. How much am I spending?
4. How strong are my safety nets?

There are no wrong answers to the questions asked during a financial physical.

There are no wrong answers to these questions. Couples should be able to work jointly on their assessment without fear of criticism, condemnation, or conflict. The worksheet on pages 68–69 will help you honestly evaluate your responses and arrive at an accurate assessment of your individual situation.

What Do I Owe? Most Americans have more debts than they do assets. Sadly, this is not due so much to big-ticket items such as a home mortgage as it is to a hefty load of smaller things like installment and credit-card debt. Over time, the balance sheet only gets more lopsided as these debt-financed purchases decrease in value.

The good news is that, so far, most people are blissfully unaware of their situation. And even if they do suspect something is out of order, the prevalent attitude is far from fatalistic. By and large, today's "debt generation" does not seem to be bothered by individual deficits.

The late Lewis Grizzard wrote a column for our Atlanta paper. He told the story of a former coworker who received a letter from one of his creditors:

> **By openly admitting how much you owe, you can take a hopeful approach to the future.**

"They're mad about the fact that I missed a payment," he said.

"The way I pay my bills is I put them all in a hat. Then I reach into the hat without looking and pull out a bill.

"I keep doing that until I'm out of money. There are always a few bills left in the hat, but at least everybody I owe has the same chance of being pulled out of the hat.

"I wrote the people back and told them if they sent me another nasty letter I wouldn't even put them in the hat anymore." (*Atlanta Journal* June 24, 1990)

As painful as it may seem at first, we need to confront our indebtedness. No financial physical is complete without an honest picture of the liabilities column. Even if your situation seems overwhelming, this step cannot be overlooked. By openly admitting how much you owe, you can take a hopeful—rather than hopeless—approach to the future.

Use the following schedules to tally your debts. The first chart is only for credit-card debt; the second chart should include all other debts (except home-mortgage debt). Before we begin, a few definitions may help:

- **Creditor:** Who you owe.
- **Initial amount borrowed:** The amount borrowed at the beginning of the loan.
- **Current balance due:** The amount of money you initially borrowed less any payments you have made against the loan; the amount you currently owe on the loan.
- **Minimum monthly payment:** The smallest monthly payment your creditor will allow without causing your account to be considered delinquent.

Credit-Card Schedule Worksheet

Date: _____

	Creditor	Current Balance	Minimum Monthly Payment	Interest Rate	Past Due? Yes or No	Comments
1.						
2.						
3.						
4.						
5.						
6.						
7.						

Credit-Card Schedule Worksheet *(Cont'd)*

	Creditor	Current Balance	Minimum Monthly Payment	Interest Rate	Past Due? Yes or No	Comments
8.						
9.						
10.						
11.						
12.						
13.						
14.						
15.						
16.						
17.						
18.						
	Totals			**NA**	**NA**	**NA**

Debt Schedule Worksheet

Date: _____

(This schedule should include car loans, loans from friends, equity lines of credit, secured and unsecured loans, life-insurance loans, etc.)

	Creditor	Initial Amount	Current Balance	Interest Rate	Past Due? Yes or No	Remaining Payments	Monthly Payment
1.							
2.							
3.							
4.							
5.							
6.							
7.							
8.							

Creditor	Initial Amount	Current Balance	Interest Rate	Past Due? Yes or No	Remaining Payments	Monthly Payment
9.						
10.						
11.						
12.						
13.						
14.						
15.						
16.						
17.						
18.						
Totals			NA	NA	NA	

What Do I Own? Most people do not really know what they own. It is a good idea, even if only for insurance purposes, to have a well-documented listing of your possessions, both on paper and through photographs or videotape. Proverbs 27:23 admonishes us to "Be diligent to know the state of your flocks, / And attend to your herds."

As a note of caution, though, this inventory must not be directed by pride. An eagerness to practice good stewardship—rather than a vain wish to review and revel in our possessions—must be our motivating desire. Do not forget the example of King David. When he pridefully instructed his army commanders to go out and count all the fighting men, he reaped God's wrath in the form of a plague that killed seventy thousand of his countrymen (2 Sam. 24).

Our firm often asks new clients to take stock of what they own using a questionnaire similar to the following form. Completing the inventory is not as difficult as it may seem; items such as silverware, jewelry, or clothing may be categorized simply as "household goods." As you work through this form, determine the worth of your assets based on their fair market value—the amount an objective, independent person would pay for this asset.

Once you have determined the sum total of your assets, subtract your debts to figure your net worth. Should your net worth turn out to be a negative number, take heart: Most Americans are in the same boat! With competent money management, though, your net worth will grow—even in times of economic uncertainty.

Determining Your Net Worth Worksheet

Date: _____

ASSETS	
Liquid	
1. Cash and checking accounts	
2. Savings accounts	
3. Money-market funds	
4. Individual stocks	
5. Individual bonds	
6. Mutual funds	
7. Cash value of life insurance	
8. CDs	
9. Other	
10. Other	
11. Total liquid assets (add lines 1–10)	
Nonliquid	
12. Rental property	
13. Home	

ASSETS *(Cont'd)*	
Nonliquid *(Cont'd)*	
14. Loans made to others	
15. Business valuation	
16. Total nonliquid assets (add lines 12–15)	
Retirement	
17. IRAs	
18. Profit sharing / pension / 401K plans	
19. Other	
20. Total retirement (add lines 17–19)	
Personal	
21. Cars	
22. Boats	
23. Furniture	
24. Household goods	
25. Total personal (add lines 21–24)	
26. **Total assets** (add lines 11, 16, 20, 25)	
DEBTS	
27. Credit-card schedule	
28. Debt schedule	
29. Home mortgage	
30. Rental-property mortgage	
31. Other	
32. **Total debt** (add lines 27–31)	
33. **Net worth** (line 26 minus line 32)	

How Much Am I Spending? Once you have determined your net worth, you need to get a handle on how fast that amount is growing—or shrinking. To do this, you must track your spending patterns to see where—and how fast—the money goes.

One couple who uses our firm for investment counseling got into an argument over the wife's spending habits. Her assessment of the situation differed markedly from her husband's. "The problem is not my overspending," she told him. "It's your under-depositing!"

Another man I heard about reacted with disbelief when he learned that one of his friends used a money-in-the-envelope system to budget for things like groceries, clothing, and entertainment. "You are kidding me!" the fellow exclaimed. "I just reach into my pocket. If there's anything in there when I pull out my hand, that's what I spend!"

Men and women fall into the same spending trap. More often than not, the problem is fueled by unexpected, impulse purchases. By taking stock of our actual spending patterns, we discover how much of the outflow is going toward regular, predictable expenses such as housing and utilities, and how much is spent on spur-of-the-moment "must-have purchases" such as that irresistible new party dress or those nifty space-age stereo speakers.

Chapter 6 offers a detailed plan for spending smart. For now, though, you can get a "big-picture" perspective on your purchasing habits by saving receipts and credit-card statements. Go through your checkbook register. Keep track of all of your expenses over a one- to three-month period. The information you glean may surprise you; certainly it will prove useful for pinpointing patterns and correcting any problems you discover.

How Strong Are My Safety Nets? Your safety nets are the things that would enable you to withstand some type of catastrophe. Life and disability insurance, healthcare coverage, and property and casualty policies are essential parts of your total safety package.

The following worksheet is designed to help you perform a preliminary assessment of your insurance needs. Once you have completed the worksheet, check with a reputable insurance adviser to see if your safety nets have any holes. Also, plan to periodically review all of your insurance coverage as your family size and needs change. Your policies' limits may be too high or too low; provision must be made for adequate—but not excessive—coverage.

Life Insurance Needs Analysis*

Income Goals for the Family		
Living expenses[1]		_____
Taxes		_____
Giving		_____
Total Income Needed	**A**	_____
Sources of Income[2]		
Social Security		_____
Pension or retirement plans		_____
Annuities or trusts		_____
Investment income[3]		_____
Spouse working		_____
Other		_____
Total Income Available	**B**	_____
Additional Income Needed (per year)[4]	**B − A = C**	_____
Insurance Required to Provide Income[5] (additional income needed × 10)	**C × 10 = D**	_____
Additional Funds Needed		
Funeral costs		_____
Debt repayment		_____
Estate tax and settlement expense		_____
Education costs		_____
Major purchases		_____
_____		_____
Total Additional Funds Needed	**E**	_____

Life Insurance Needs Analysis* *(Cont'd)*

Insurance Needed[6]	**E + D = F**	_____
Assets Available for Sale		
Real estate		_____
Stocks, bonds, other investments		_____
Savings available (to meet needs listed above)[7]		_____
_____		_____
_____		_____
Total from Sale of Assets	**G**	_____
Total Insurance Needed[8]	**F − G = H**	_____
Insurance available now	**I**	_____
Additional Insurance Needed	**H − I = J**	_____

Notes

1. Use 80% of present annual living expenses.
2. Income anticipated on a regular basis.
3. Income from investments not liquidated.
4. The income needed less the income available (B − A = C).
5. This assumes the life insurance proceeds could be invested at 10% and provide the needed amounts. The investment percentage may be contingent on economic conditions or investment knowledge. The multiplication factor is 1 divided by the percentage return on insurance proceeds.

    Example: $10\% = 1/.10 = 10; 8\% = 1/.08 = 12.5; 12\% = 1/.12 = 8.33$

6. Insurance needed is the sum of insurance required to provide income (D) plus additional funds needed (E).
7. Savings available would be only that part of savings that could be applied to meet the needs listed above. It would not include the savings needed to meet family living goals.
8. Total insurance needed is the insurance needed less the amount available from the sale of assets (F − G = H).

NOTE: No adjustment has been made in these calculations for inflation. If you feel that you can earn 10% but that will be eroded by 3–4% inflation, then you should use 6–7% rather than 10% in calculating D, the amount of insurance required to provide income. This will increase the amount of insurance needed. You can use any investment or inflation assumption you would like.

How to Plan Your Life Insurance Program (Atlanta: Ronald Blue & Co., 1987) 18–19.

LET YOUR LIGHT SHINE

All four of the steps we have covered—determining how much you owe, how much you own, how much you spend, and how well you are protected—are essential to a thorough and complete financial physical. Once you have an accurate picture of your situation, you can set goals and plan to achieve them.

The financial physical is an indispensable prerequisite to your financial-planning process. Like Joseph, you must travel throughout your entire "land" to get a well-defined picture of the situation. And like Joseph, if you begin at the beginning and take care to set goals and follow a wise and proper plan, you will reap the benefits of successful stewardship.

You will not be the only one who benefits from this process. The famine in Joseph's day extended throughout the world, and nowhere could any food be found except in Egypt. Joseph threw open the store-houses, selling grain to Egyptians and foreigners alike. The entire world descended on Egypt, turning to Joseph and his abundant provisions to meet their desperate need.

> **The financial physical is an indispensable prerequisite to your financial-planning process.**

Through it all, Joseph never forgot the Lord. He credited God with bringing him to Egypt, making him a ruler over the land, and saving lives during the terrible famine.

Like Joseph, we also have the opportunity to direct the world's eyes toward the Lord. As we prosper during times of economic uncertainty, people will be drawn to us for answers. Our proactive approach, demonstrated through wise financial stewardship, will attract attention. As Jesus instructed us in Matthew 5:16, we can let our light shine before men, that they may see our good deeds and praise our Father in heaven.

The world is watching. Will you be like Joseph? In the next chapter you will learn how to develop your own financial strategy by setting goals and planning how to achieve them. As you do, remember, God gave you the perspective, the guidelines, and the wisdom to enjoy prosperity and peace—even when facing an economically uncertain future.

5

Step 2: Develop Your Finish Lines

Not long ago I came upon a list of goals Judy and I had written in 1978. Newcomers to Atlanta, we had juggled the challenges of adjusting to a new job in a new city with the parenting responsibilities that abounded in our growing family. Our fifth child had just been born.

Judy and I were still relatively new Christians, and we wanted, more than anything, to put our faith into action by making appropriate lifestyle and financial decisions. Recognizing that our lives needed some concrete direction, we took off on a goal-setting weekend. By Sunday afternoon we had shaped and molded our priorities into thirty-six clearly defined objectives. Among them were the desires to eliminate debt, increase our giving, provide a quality education for our children, and enjoy several specific vacation and entertainment dreams.

That was more than fifteen years ago. Since then Judy and I have reviewed and revised our goals through repeated goal-setting getaways. As I glanced through the pages of our initial effort in 1978, I realized how little our goals and values have changed over the years. For example, we still place items such as providing for our children and giving to the Lord's work at or near the top of our priority lists.

Your goals will reflect your own values, and the goals you set will naturally dictate and define your behavior. Thus, aiming at the right targets becomes vitally important if you hope to enjoy a life of fulfillment, peace, and prosperity.

Your goals will reflect your own values.

Setting goals, I have found, is a lot like taking a financial physical. The very prospect of undergoing a physical, for example, can motivate you to improve your financial health. Likewise, the mere act of defining a goal puts you that much closer to achieving it.

When I underwent my Cooper Clinic physical at age forty, sheer vanity compelled me to begin getting in shape even before any tests were performed. Afterward, I easily identified several very logical goals: eating right, getting proper exercise, and scheduling periodic checkups. They quickly became part of my regular routine.

The mere act of defining a goal puts you that much closer to achieving it.

Other goals required more thought and planning. I resolved to learn to snow ski before I turned fifty, and I began shouldering my golf bag again for another crack at the links. Both sports now figure prominently in my leisure time. The point is that setting goals—and planning how to achieve them—came as a natural outgrowth of the physical evaluation process.

In the last chapter you took your financial physical. Based on that assessment, you can now set goals that will provide direction, motivation, and discipline in your financial life. These benefits make goal setting an integral part of any endeavor. In times of economic uncertainty, however, having a series of carefully considered and well-defined objectives takes on added significance. Goals and dreams that are taken for granted during periods of prosperity may require a new strategy or additional effort when times are tough.

THE GOALS YOU NEED TO
SURVIVE AND THRIVE

In my book *Master Your Money*, I recounted the story of John Goddard, the man who "wanted to do it all." As a fifteen-year-old boy, Goddard made a list of 127 lifetime goals, including exploring the Nile, climbing Mount Everest, visiting the moon, and starring in a Tarzan movie. When *Master Your Money* was first published, Goddard had completed 106 of his 127 goals.

His approach—thinking big and listing every dream, no matter how impractical or remote—reflects a shotgun strategy. As you consider your financial future—especially in light of economic uncertainty—you will want to focus your sights on a series of narrower targets.

Review the results of your financial physical. As you weigh your position, ask yourself some difficult questions:

- Do I need to accelerate debt repayment?
- Am I financially flexible enough to handle the loss of a job or an investment?
- Does my spending reflect concern over economic uncertainty—or am I presuming upon the future?

- How risk-proof are my investments? What do I depend on them for?
- Have I planned for future taxes? If I had to sell an investment, could I meet the tax obligations?

Questions like these help sharpen your perspective on your financial circumstances. They also serve as the foundation for the following five-step process that allows you to create a roster of clearly defined, target-oriented goals.

Five Steps to Good Goals

1. **List your goals.** Psalm 37:4 says, "Delight yourself also in the LORD, / And He shall give you the desires of your heart." If you trust Him to do so, God promises to put the right desires in your heart. Working from this perspective, make a list of your financial dreams and goals. Perhaps you want to start your own business or retire in a place near your grandchildren. Maybe you have two children to put through college. Or maybe you want to be able to enjoy a truly relaxing vacation with your spouse. Would you like to get away? What about those piano or tennis lessons the kids want—have you figured out how to pay for them?

Let your imagination wander. Consider which goals are apt to require financial forethought. As you reflect, ask God to help you establish objectives that will give your life purpose and direction.

The list of suggestions included in the Goal-Setting Weekend Agenda at the conclusion of this chapter may help you think through your needs and desires. Having

prayerfully considered your goals, make a list of everything you would like to achieve, from career hopes to
vacation dreams to savings plans.

My Goals and Dreams

Date: _____

1. (For example, increase savings) _____
2. (For example, build liquidity) _____
3. _____
4. _____
5. _____
6. _____
7. _____
8. _____
9. _____
10. _____
11. _____
12. _____
13. _____
14. _____
15. _____
16. _____
17. _____
18. _____
19. _____
20. _____

2. **Consolidate and refine.** You have made your list;
now check it twice. See if there are things that you have
unintentionally jotted down more than once. Perhaps, as
in the example above, you listed "increase savings" and
"build liquidity." You may be able to blend these goals into
just one objective. The idea is to refine your list so that it
reflects a roster of clearly stated, distinct goals.

Consolidated Goals and Dreams

Date: _____

1. (For example, build liquidity by saving more) _____
2. _____
3. _____
4. _____
5. _____
6. _____
7. _____
8. _____
9. _____
10. _____
11. _____
12. _____
13. _____
14. _____
15. _____

3. **Prioritize.** Some of your goals will obviously be more important than others. Using your consolidated list, evaluate each goal and place it into one of the following categories:

a. Indispensable goals. Examples of "must-do" goals include getting out of bankruptcy or providing for a sick child. Economically, and in some cases physically, the items in this category pertain to your very survival.

1. _____
2. _____
3. _____

b. Important goals. These may include objectives such as buying a home, providing for retirement, or sending a child to college. The things on this list will be high priorities, yet they are not absolutely vital to your survival.

1. _____
2. _____
3. _____

c. Likes and wants. This category is for your desires. Perhaps you are eager to increase your giving percentage, or maybe you want to save for a family vacation. Those kinds of goals fit here.

1. _____

2. _____

3. _____

d. Future dreams. This list is your chance to think big. Do you hope to own your own business someday? Is your heart's desire to go into full-time Christian work—even if it means saying good-bye to your salary? Have you always wanted to take an extended tour through Europe? Economic uncertainty may make dreams like these seem remote, but do not discard them—particularly if your dream is one you feel God has put on your heart.

1. _____

2. _____

3. _____

e. Goals that others think you should have. The final grouping on your list is for those things that other people think you need. You may not agree with the life insurance salesman who thinks you should increase your coverage. You may not see the urgency your mother does when she begs you to settle down and buy a home. You may think your wife is just not visionary enough when she advises you to get out of debt and start saving some money. Even so, if the goal seems even remotely logical or legitimate to you, write it down for consideration.

1. _____

2. _____

3. _____

Your individual financial structure will dictate how you group your objectives. Someone who has a number of high-risk investments, for example, may need to put debt repayment or liquidity-building into the "indispensable" category, while someone with little or no debt may consider building liquidity merely as an "important" goal. Likewise, buying a new car may be "important" for the woman whose job depends on reliable transportation while the purchase is only a "want" for the man who is just plain tired of driving his ugly, old clunker.

Once you have listed and categorized your goals, pick

your top five priorities. Your list may include twenty-five or fifty objectives; you cannot possibly pursue all or even most of them. Narrow your choices to the five most pressing concerns.

This selection process forces you to examine your priorities. Your choices will undoubtedly be driven by your value system and your financial circumstances, and thus your decisions may be marked by tension, especially as you juggle short- and long-term goals.

Suppose, for example, that your resources are limited and you want to save a substantial amount to send your child to college. You are also dying to get away for a much-needed weekend alone with your spouse. Both goals are legitimate. One is a long-term objective. The other is a short-term desire . . . yet the health of your marriage today will have long-term consequences. It is up to you to weigh the options; sacrificing something will almost always be necessary.

Top Five Goals

Date: _____

1. _____
2. _____
3. _____
4. _____
5. _____

4. Quantify your five goals. Once you have selected your five top priorities, define them in numeric terms. A goal may take a certain amount of time or require a set amount of money. If you cannot quantify a goal, you cannot pursue it effectively.

I wanted to learn to snow ski before my fiftieth birthday; that goal established the time frame I had to work in. Likewise, when Judy and I set those goals in 1978, we purposed to increase our charitable giving to more than 15 percent of our income each year. By attaching a numerical percentage to our desire to give, we could recognize and press toward the finish line.

If you want to pay for a college education, figure out how much it will cost and how long you have to save the necessary funds. If going into full-time Christian ministry is one of your top priorities, how much—if any—money will you need to make up for a salary cutback? What percentage of your living expenses will need to come from investment income? Be as specific as you can as you quantify and define your goals.

Top Five Goals—Quantified

(For example: Save seventy-five dollars per month for a family vacation next summer.)
1. _____
2. _____
3. _____
4. _____
5. _____

5. **Keep your goals visible.** Your goals must be seen easily and often if you hope to stay on the right track. I keep a notebook that includes all the goals that Judy and I have ever written. Others post goals on car dashboards, by kitchen sinks, inside checkbook covers—anywhere they will be seen and remembered. Wallace Johnson, the highly successful cofounder of Holiday Inn, always kept a list of

his top ten priorities on a three-by-five card attached to his bathroom mirror.

<table>
<tr><td>

Setting goals is an ongoing process.

</td><td>

In addition to keeping your goals visible, you must also plan to take an even closer look at them from time to time. A periodic review is necessary to see which goals need to be revised or eliminated, where

</td></tr>
</table>

additions might need to be made, and which goals may be happily checked off the list and moved into the "accomplishments" category.

Setting goals is an ongoing process. You will want to make new lists from time to time, and while your values are apt to remain basically unchanged, chances are your financial circumstances will vary. This shift may make certain goals more—or less—attainable. It will create a new set of financial needs, and as a result, your priorities and goals may differ from month to month, year to year, or decade to decade.

HUSBANDS AND WIVES: SETTING GOALS YOU BOTH CAN LIVE WITH

In the last section I noted the tension that can occur when you have to juggle short- and long-term objectives. Another potential hot spot is when husbands and wives try to agree on the goals they need to pursue jointly. The mere attempt at effective communication is enough to stop many couples at or near the drawing board.

To cope with this inevitable tension, I recommend at least one annual getaway weekend. Goal setting may be the weekend's ultimate purpose, yet the benefits of such a concentrated time together will inevitably spill over into the relationship itself.

For men, the prospect of two or three days devoted primarily to communicating with their wives is often daunting. What seems perfectly natural in a professional environment—setting goals, discussing plans openly with coworkers, even going on retreats to formulate business strategy—suddenly poses an unfamiliar threat in a one-on-one, husband-wife situation. Communication necessitates vulnerability—which means a husband's independence and status may be at stake.

I remember the early years of our marriage before I became a Christian. The last thing I wanted to do was give Judy any control over my life. I guarded my independence fiercely, never announcing in advance my plans to play golf or anything else lest she try to thwart me.

> **Communication necessitates vulnerability—which means a husband's independence and status may be at stake.**

I have come to realize that it takes a spiritually and emotionally mature man to risk giving up his own goals for the sake of the couple's goals and the betterment of his marriage. Women, on the other hand, typically welcome the communication opportunity that a goal-setting weekend presents.

For a woman, the discussion of goals provides direction in the marriage, which is a cornerstone of her deepest need for security. Getting her husband to communicate is a giant step toward getting him to assume responsibility and leadership in the household.

As I mentioned earlier, Judy and I have worked our way through several goal-setting weekends, and we have learned that we each must be committed to establishing *our* goals, rather than creating a matching set of his-and-her objectives. We also recognize that, as we brainstorm through our goals, there are never any right or wrong suggestions. There is no need to "win"; rather, we try to come to an agreement in those areas where our thoughts and dreams diverge.

While you may fear the differences of opinion or mismatched priorities that will inevitably be spotlighted by a goal-setting weekend, consider the benefits. In acknowledging your spouse's values and priorities, goals that you once overlooked or forgot may come to the fore and captivate your attention. Reluctant as I am to admit it, I never even considered focusing on our children's education as a goal until I saw it on Judy's list. Of course that was a priority—I only wish I had thought of it first!

> **I cannot overstate the importance of prioritizing and clearly defining your goals.**

While our weekends are rarely very structured, Judy and I have developed a sort of routine that allows for a good amount of reflection, communication, and relaxation. At the end of this chapter I have included a typical schedule and some notes from our times together. Feel free to follow this plan or use it as a springboard to create your own agenda. (Dave and Claudia Arp's book *The Ultimate Marriage Builder* also provides ideas for a weekend that will enrich your marriage and quantify your goals.)

Use the suggested goal-setting topics plus the worksheets from this chapter as you work toward setting goals you both want to pursue. I cannot overstate the importance of prioritizing and clearly defining your goals. With a concrete task in mind, you will flourish; without one, you will flounder—regardless of how financially secure your personal picture may appear. Consider, for example, the lives of two prominent men in the Old Testament: Nehemiah and Solomon.

A TALE OF TWO BUILDERS

Nehemiah was an able statesman and a patriotic Jew. Upon learning that the wall around Jerusalem had been destroyed, Nehemiah responded immediately with mourning, fasting, and prayer. Then, with the king's permission, he established a timetable and traveled to Jerusalem to see what could be done to repair the city.

Like Joseph when he set out to secure Egypt's survival, Nehemiah began his job with a reconnaissance mission. He kept his inspection of the city a secret, taking only a few men out to examine the damage under the cover of darkness. Then, having accurately assessed the situation, he established a goal and addressed his fellow Jews: "You see the distress that we are in, how Jerusalem lies waste, and its gates are burned with fire. Come and let us build the wall of Jerusalem, that we may no longer be a reproach" (Neh. 2:17).

Nehemiah's example offers several characteristics of effective goal setting:

1. Nehemiah began with prayer and continued to seek the Lord's favor and guidance at every juncture.
2. Nehemiah could not see the final result, nor did he know exactly how the task was to be accomplished, yet he set a goal and got started in a specific direction.
3. Nehemiah's goal was quantifiable. He told the king exactly how long he planned to be gone, and then he defined the job to exact specifications. He did

not say, "Come, let us rebuild as much as we can." Rather, he commissioned his men to "build the wall of Jerusalem."

Openly ridiculed by their enemies, Nehemiah and his workers pressed on to complete their mission—even under the constant threat of an attack by outside troublemakers. Thanks to his careful, prayerful approach, Nehemiah was able to overcome tremendous opposition and succeed where others had failed miserably. As a result, the entire project was completed in an unbelievable fifty-two days.

Nehemiah's accomplishment was remarkable— yet, at first glance, it might seem to pale in comparison to Solomon's building programs. Reputed to be the wisest man alive, Solomon drew crowds from all over the world. People came to hear him speak—and to view his incredible wealth. All of his household goods were made of gold, from the shields to the goblets. His throne was an astonishing work of intricate luxury. His commercial ventures became legendary, and his fleet of trading ships, chariots, and horses spread his fame around the world.

Yet Solomon was not satisfied. Even his greatest enterprise—building the elaborate temple in Jerusalem—failed to provide any lasting sense of accomplishment. In the book of Ecclesiastes, which is commonly attributed to Solomon, the oft-repeated refrain is that "Everything is vanity"; in other words, everything is meaningless. Worldly pleasures, hard work, and even great riches amount to nothing, Solomon wrote. "He who loves silver will not be satisfied with silver; nor he who loves abundance, with increase" (Eccles. 5:10).

The truth in these words, written near the end of

Solomon's life, indicates that he eventually woke up to his misplaced ambitions. For the majority of his reign, however, Solomon's primary financial focus seemed to be rooted simply in building and accumulating. The building of wealth became an end in itself—and as Solomon ultimately discovered, the pursuit of riches offered no lasting gratification.

Nehemiah had a quantifiable, tangible task. Solomon did not. Nehemiah enjoyed the satisfaction of realizing his goal in a remarkably short time. Solomon, on the other hand, never had a finish line. As wealthy as he was, he floundered in frustration and the futility of meaningless riches.

Solomon never had a finish line.

As Solomon learned, financial security and satisfaction are not rooted in income level or material achievements. Nor are they exclusively a by-product of prosperous or stable economic times. By focusing on the right set of goals, you can build a secure financial future—even if, like Nehemiah, your "Jerusalem" lies, for the moment, in ruins.

As Solomon learned, financial security and satisfaction are not rooted in income level or material achievements.

By establishing a finish line, you will avoid the temptation to pursue the meaningless riches Solomon described as "vanity." Your goals will keep you on track, and with the direction and motivation they provide, you can look forward to the peace of mind, sense of fulfillment, and ultimate security that come with knowing you have provided a storm shelter for your family's financial future.

Goal-Setting Weekend Agenda:
A Tool for Husbands and Wives

Remember: This is not a hard-and-fast schedule. It is simply a plan that has stood the test of time and experience in our lives. Feel free to make revisions to suit your individual needs, but remember to allow plenty of time for quality communication.

Friday Evening

Start your weekend with an unstructured evening. Make no attempt to start setting goals; instead, just enjoy talking with your spouse over a relaxing dinner, a leisurely walk, or some other communication-fostering activity.

Take time to pray together, even if praying with your husband or wife is a new or unfamiliar activity. The goal-setting process must be grounded in prayer; otherwise, it becomes merely an exercise in wishful thinking or selfish dreaming. Make this focus on prayer the backbone of the entire weekend.

Saturday Morning

Take time apart from one another to set goals as outlined in the "how-to" section of this chapter. Use the worksheets on pages 79–83 if you need help or direction. Do it all—from listing your hopes and dreams to categorizing and quantifying the goals. The only step you should omit is selecting your five top-priority goals; this is a step you and your spouse will work on together.

LUNCH BREAK

Saturday Afternoon

With your lists in hand, get together with your spouse and compare notes. This can be a real eye-opening time. Judy and I usually agree on 70 to 80 percent of our goals; we tend to spend most of our time in this session discussing the other 20 or 30 percent. Remember, there are no right or wrong answers. Use this time as an opportunity to recognize and appreciate one another's priorities.

Saturday Evening

Relax. You have done a lot of work, and you may feel mentally or emotionally drained. Saturday evening should be a chance for the information you have garnered to "simmer," while you and your spouse take time simply to enjoy one another.

Sunday Morning

This is the fun—and challenging—part. Remembering that a goal-setting weekend is not a time to establish "my" or "your" goals, prepare to come up with a list of "our" goals. Pick no more than ten objectives.

Next, be sure that these goals are well defined, and try to quantify them. Wherever possible, set times, dates, or amounts that will let you know when you've accomplished each goal.

Armed with a list of five to ten goals you and your spouse have agreed to pursue together, you are now ready to establish a strategy for accomplishing them. Congratulations: You have already done the hardest part!

Goal-Setting Topics
A Catalog of Ideas to Get You Started

Savings Goals
- How much do we need?
- How should we save? Weekly? Monthly? Annual bonus?
- Why? What are we saving for?

Debt Goals
- How much is okay?
- Should we avoid it altogether?
- Should we get out of it?

Lifestyle Goals
- What kind of house do we need or want?
- Do we want to take a vacation? Where?
- What about areas like entertainment, clothing, etc.?

Education Goals for Children or Self
- Public or private schooling?
- College? University?
- Trade school?

Vacation Goals
- How many this year?
- Where to go?
- With kids? Without?

Insurance Goals
- Life, home, health, auto, other?
- How much do we need?
- What kind of policy suits our needs?

Giving Goals
- How much to give?
- Where to give?
- When to give? Weekly? Biweekly? Monthly?

Tax Goals
- Do we need to reduce our taxes?
- How can we manage them?
- Do we under-withhold?
- Overwithhold?

Family Goals
- Special needs for aging parents? Disabilities? A gifted child?
- Family time: When? What? How? Where? Why?
- One-on-one time with children?

Marriage Goals
- Date nights?
- Intimacy?
- Communication needs?

Career Goals
- Starting a business?
- Advancement?
- Job satisfaction? Location?

Children
- How many?
- Spacing?
- When to start a family?

Household Goals
- When, where, and what kind of home to buy/rent?
- Furniture needed?
- Special needs: room for guests, home office, etc.?

Investment Goals
- Where to invest?
- Why invest?
- How much to invest?

6

Step 3:
Prepare a
Spending Plan

I was a junior at Indiana University when several buddies and I decided to spend the coming summer on Waikiki Beach. As none of us came from wealthy families, we each had to scrounge our way to Hawaii. I hitchhiked to California, then found a "nonscheduled" (i.e. cheap) flight to the islands.

I will never forget our first moments near the ocean. How many surfboards should we buy? Would we need two motor scooters or four? As my friends and I stood in the warm island sunshine, the possibilities seemed limitless.

It only took one week before we were forced to rethink our perspective. There were no jobs to be found. With no work and no money, we resorted to combing the beach for spare change dropped by the sunbathers. Our sand-sifting netted enough nickels and dimes to buy groceries. We survived—but there were no surfboards or motor scooters.

Poking around in the sand to find extra money is one way to survive financially. A much quicker way, however, is to simply reduce living expenses. It may take less mental effort or discipline to sift along a beach, but as one who has tried both methods, I can safely say that curtailing your spending is a far more effective means of securing the cash you need.

A disciplined spending strategy is critical to achieving and maintaining fiscal fitness.

People may talk about cutting back—but the truth is that most of us (95 percent) spend as much money as we earn or even more. The key to a smart and successful spending plan, however, is to spend less than you earn and consequently gain more financial freedom and flexibility. It does not matter whether you make ten thousand dollars a year or one hundred thousand dollars; a disciplined spending strategy is critical to achieving and maintaining fiscal fitness.

By echoing this refrain throughout this book, my challenge to you is to develop a proactive approach and take control of your finances. You have already taken your financial physical and set some specific goals; now you must evaluate your income, develop a budget, and come up with a plan that will enable you to reach your financial finish lines. This process will probably involve hard work, careful planning, and a good deal of self-discipline, but smart spending is never an impossible task.

THE REWARDS OF SMART SPENDING

Spending less than you earn is the commonsense key to living within your income. Nobody plans to overspend. On the contrary, most of us aim to make room in the budget for the things we know are important, such as saving and tithing. What happens, though, is that we fail to budget or plan properly, and we come up short when it's time to pay the bills.

Savings and tithes are often the first casualties. Next, we use credit cards when we face a cash shortfall, reasoning that we can make it up in a month or so. Then, as we slip further and further behind, we give in to the temptation to make only the minimum payment required on the cards.

In this precarious position, our wallets are no match for an unexpected calamity when it comes along. A major car repair, a medical emergency, a leaking roof, or a broken water pipe—any one of a thousand sudden needs can catapult us into debt with astonishing force. Peering into our five- or ten-thousand-dollar hole of debt, we teeter on the edge of disaster and wonder, "How in the world did I get here?"

As common as they are, the financial problems associated with unforeseen or unbudgeted expenses are actually fairly simple to prevent. The strategy is to make sure that your income exceeds your outflow—even in the face of unexpected expenses. Following this rule opens the door to several significant benefits:

1. Spending less than you earn eliminates the possibility of debt. A person who spends less than he or she earns creates margin—the cash reserve that provides protection from the storms of economic uncertainty. Job losses, investment downturns, and even relatively minor mishaps such as broken pipes or car repairs can drive even the best-intentioned money manager into debt if no savings margin exists.

2. Spending less than you earn makes saving

money possible. The standard pecking order for most budgets looks something like this:

> Lifestyle spending
> Taxes
> Debt
> Savings
> Giving

Once we divvy up our paychecks for everything from clothing to entertainment, we squeeze out enough to cover taxes and make the payments on our debts—not because we want to but because we have to. Finally, the leftovers—if there are any—are begrudgingly parceled out to savings, and finally to tithing.

By flipping this order upside down, however, we achieve a biblical—and successful—spending plan:

> Giving
> Savings
> Debt
> Taxes
> Lifestyle spending

Setting the right priorities is an integral part of controlling your spending, and by following this giving-and-saving-first spending plan, chances are good that you will never get into financial trouble. Moreover, you will be able to rack up significant savings—again, establishing yourself in a strong position to meet an unpredictable future.

3. Spending less than you earn eliminates the possibility of future financial problems. Because smart spending eliminates the debt option and creates a legitimate savings plan, the longer you follow this practice, the less likely it is that you will encounter severe financial hardship in the future.

I know of a man named Jim who was laid off from his six-figure management position and remained jobless for more than a year. With two children to put through college, the family's future might have been grim—yet Jim had long practiced frugality in everything from clipping coupons to buying a modest home to setting aside money in an education fund. With little or no debt and a carefully tended nest egg, Jim countered the blow of unemployment and survived far better than most.

Eliminating the possibility of debt, saving money, and establishing a secure financial position for the future sounds like an ideal—but impractical or impossible—objective. Yet it is actually a relatively straightforward task, provided you follow a sound financial plan. Spending money is easy; knowing how to do it right takes common sense, discipline, and occasionally, a few tricks from the files of folks who have taken control of their finances and learned how to stretch a dollar in both good times and bad. The following sections describe some of those tricks.

THE HOW-TO'S OF SMART SPENDING

Anyone who has ever tried to live on a budget knows that the process requires both dedication and discipline.

Before you can begin to control your spending, however, you must recognize exactly how much money you have available. You must accurately evaluate your spendable income.

Evaluating Your Spendable Income

A family making thirty thousand dollars per year does not have thirty thousand dollars to spend. Assuming a tithe of 10 percent and tax withholdings of about 20 percent, the family is left with no more than twenty-one thousand dollars to cover everything from housing, food, and clothing to entertainment, car repairs, medical expenses, and more. And that does not include any savings! Add outstanding debt to the list, and the belt gets even tighter.

Only about 50 or 60 percent of your paycheck can be considered discretionary income.

The fact is that only about 50 or 60 percent of your total paycheck can be considered discretionary income. To get an accurate picture of your individual spending resources, begin by completing the Projected Annual Income worksheet, which follows. Before you begin, a few notes may help:

- The Amount Received Monthly column is for regular, monthly cash inflow. Use the Amount Received Annually column to record money you receive other than monthly, such as tax refunds or cash gifts.
- When calculating your estimated interest and dividends, refer to your prior year's tax return and to your net-worth statement (see the Determining

Your Net Worth Worksheet in Chapter 4). For example, if you have two thousand dollars in a money-market fund that will earn approximately 4 percent annually, you should record eighty dollars in estimated interest from that fund. If you have rental property, estimate your annual rental income, then subtract your annual expenses (including your mortgage payment) to arrive at a net cash-flow amount.

Projected Annual Income

Year: _____

Income Sources:	Amount Received Monthly	Amount Received Annually	Annual Amount
Gross wages (husband)			
Gross wages (wife)			
Business income			
Baby-sitting income			
Pension income			
Miscellaneous income			
Rental property, net			
Interest			
Interest			
Dividends			
Dividends from mutual funds			
Gifts			
Total Gross Income			

Having calculated your total gross income, you can figure out how much money you actually have available for spending. Following the biblical spending model described earlier, make allowance first for annual giving totals, then savings, then debt retirement, and finally, taxes.

Annual Spendable Income

1. Total gross income (from Projected Annual Income worksheet)	
2. Charitable giving	
3. Savings	
a. Via payroll deduction	
b. Personal	
4. Debt repayment	
a. Credit cards (per month × 12)	
b. Car payments (per month × 12)	
c. Other	
5. Taxes	
a. Federal withholdings	
b. State withholdings	
c. FICA withholdings	
d. Current year federal estimates	
e. Current year state estimates	
f. Prior year taxes	
6. Total (Add lines 2–5)	
7. Total spendable income (line 1 minus line 6)	

Developing a Spending Plan

Having evaluated your spendable income, the first step in developing a successful spending plan is to determine how much you have actually been spending in the past. Next, decide how much you would like to spend on a monthly basis in the future. This process—known as living on a budget—takes self-discipline, realism, and a long-term commitment.

George is a fellow who works in our office. He used to play professional football, and while he would never have been considered fat, he did have some leftover weightlifter's bulk he wanted to shed. He changed his eating habits, and at six-foot-four, he ultimately cut a rather dashing figure.

Meanwhile, I continued to struggle to deflate the spare tire that circled my waistline. "Why don't you look like George?" Judy teased me one day.

"I would," I hastily assured her, "if only I were seven inches taller!"

Like many people, I have no problem dropping five pounds in just a couple of days—only to gain it back again the moment I let down my guard. But I realized I did not need to lose just five pounds; I needed to take off about fifteen pounds. Recognizing the importance of setting a "big" goal and allowing ample time to achieve it, I decided to lose twenty-five pounds—and I gave myself six months to get the job done. I am happy to report that I accomplished my goal. To do it, I had to change my eating habits and adopt a long-term attitude about the task.

> **You must be realistic about what you are trying to do and give yourself enough time to finish the job.**

The same principles hold true in establishing and maintaining a budget. You need to set a worthy goal (that is, a big goal). Then you must be realistic about what you are trying to do and give yourself enough time to finish the job. Like the weight loss that results from a change in eating habits, the only permanent solution to spending woes must be fueled by a long-term shift in spending patterns.

To create a realistic spending plan, begin by answering two questions: What are you spending? and What would you like to spend? Getting the correct information can take as long as two years, but if you discipline yourself to stick with the process, your eventual budget will be better equipped to withstand the ups and downs of economic uncertainty.

1. What Are You Spending? To answer this question, go back over the last twelve to twenty-four months and gather data from checkbook registers, credit-card receipts, and other records. Remember to include automatic-teller withdrawals and checks written for cash; if you cannot remember what the money was used for, record the amounts in the miscellaneous category.

2. What Would You Like to Spend? This question reflects your first attempt to develop a budget. Ask yourself, "Given my spending history, what would I like the future to look like?" All of us would like to spend more on entertainment, clothes, etc., but we need to live within the parameters of our income. (Note: Most people underestimate how much they spend by at least 5 percent; so, **once you determine how much you want to spend, add 5 percent to each budget category to give yourself a more realistic picture.**)

The answers to these two questions provide the basis for your spending plan, which you can develop by using the following Living Expenses worksheet. In the Paid

Monthly column, record the amounts you plan to spend each month. Expenses paid other than monthly go in the Paid Annually column. Total your annual living expenses in the Total Amount column.

Your Living Expenses

Year: _____

	Actual Prior Month	Paid Monthly	Paid Annually	Total Amount
HOUSING:				
Mortgage/Rent				
Insurance				
Property taxes				
Electricity				
Heating				
Water/Sanitation				
Telephone				
Cleaning				
Repairs/Maintenance				
Supplies				
Improvements				
Furnishings				
Total housing:				
FOOD:				
CLOTHING:				
TRANSPORTATION:				
Insurance				
Gas and oil				
Maintenance and repairs				
Parking				
Other				
Total transportation:				

Your Living Expenses *(Cont'd)*

	Actual Prior Month	Paid Monthly	Paid Annually	Total Amount
ENTERTAINMENT/RECREATION:				
Eating out				
Baby-sitters				
Magazines and newspapers				
Vacation				
Clubs and activities				
Total entertainment/recreation:				
MEDICAL EXPENSES:				
Insurance				
Doctors/Dentists				
Payroll deductions				
Drugs				
Other				
Other				
Total medical:				
INSURANCE:				
Life				
Disability				
Total insurance:				
CHILDREN:				
School lunches				
Allowances				
Tuition (grade/high school)				
Tuition (college)				
Lessons				
Other				
Other				
Total children:				

	Actual Prior Month	Paid Monthly	Paid Annually	Total Amount
GIFTS:				
Christmas				
Birthdays				
Anniversary				
Other				
Other				
Total gifts:				
MISCELLANEOUS:				
Toiletries				
Husband lunches/misc.				
Wife misc.				
Dry cleaning				
Animals (licenses, food, vet)				
Beauty and barber				
Other				
Other				
Total miscellaneous:				
TOTAL LIVING EXPENSES:				

Analyzing and Adjusting Your Plan

Your Living Expenses worksheet represents your budget. Once you have attempted to live according to this spending plan for a period of time (I recommend an entire year to get an accurate picture of total spending), you will probably need to make some adjustments.

Obviously, your goal is to live within your budget so that more money comes in than goes out. By analyzing your cash flow, you can determine how much margin your budget includes. Margin is essentially extra cash; it is the amount of income received over and above your outflow.

Use the simple Cash-Flow Analysis worksheet that follows to figure your margin, both on your initial budget and then on your adjusted plan.

Cash-Flow Analysis Worksheet

	Initial Plan	Adjusted Plan
1. Total spendable income (see Annual Spendable Income worksheet total)		
2. Total living expenses (see Living Expenses worksheet total)		
3. Cash-flow margin (Line 1 minus line 2)		

If you overspend your budget, you will reduce your margin. The only way to live on a negative margin is to borrow money—which only increases your debt commitments, further reducing your margin.

Again, your goal is to live within your budget. As your income increases through salary raises or other means, your margin will increase—provided your living expenses do not change. Your margin—your extra cash—is the very thing that will enable you to take advantage of the investment strategies and options outlined later in this book.

(Note: My books *Master Your Money* and *Taming the Money Monster* offer additional information on successful spending plans. There are also a number of excellent computer programs available to help take the guesswork out of budgeting; check with your local software retailer to find out which package best meets your needs.)

ADVICE FROM THE EXPERTS

Living within your budget may seem like an overwhelming task. Yet as the specter of economic uncertainty continues to loom over our nation, more people than ever before are subscribing to the "new frugality" and taking proactive steps to control their spending. Responding to our collective sentiment, popular magazines such as *Money* and *Business Week* regularly feature how-to articles on cutting costs, spending sensibly, and making ends meet.

The following suggestions reflect only a sampling of the creative things you can do in various areas of your life to reduce your expenses and make your budget work.

Housing Costs

Refinance your home. Interest rates go up and down. In 1992 and 1993 they were very, very low. When rates are lower than your mortgage, you should consider refinancing. The rule of thumb is this: If you can lower your rate by two percentage points and you plan to stay in your house for three years or more, refinancing almost always makes sense—even if you have to pay closing costs to do it.

Trim your utility bill. Set your thermostat five degrees higher in summer and five degrees lower when winter comes. Ask your utility company about installing a load controller, which automatically shuts down or lowers power on certain appliances to conserve electricity. You can also get programmable thermostats at most hardware or home-repair shops; these devices raise and lower the temperature of your house according to your individual lifestyle needs and schedules. When Judy and I installed these, our electricity bills dropped by 15 to 20 percent!

Learn to do your own home repairs. Check out the do-it-yourself books available at most home-supply centers for everything from maintenance tips to building and repair guides.

Consider relocating. As a last resort to reduce housing costs, you may want to move to another house or even another city. Even a short move to the next town can have a dramatic impact on costs, from housing prices to taxes.

Food Bills

Join a discount or wholesale club. Groceries are just one of the myriad items available at rock-bottom prices through outlets such as BJ's, Sam's, and the Price Club. Consumer research shows that these clubs offer a 26 percent savings over standard retailers. Plus, by shopping in bulk, you can save on time and gas as you cut down on trips to the grocery store.

Plant a garden. This healthy idea can help trim food bills by as much as 30 percent, even on a relatively small plot of land.

Change your eating habits. Cut out some nonessentials such as snacks and soft drinks, and cook from scratch rather than buying prepackaged foods or dining out.

Clip coupons. With many grocery stores offering double coupons, the savings can really add up. Make clipping a family activity—but take care not to clip coupons for items you had not planned to purchase or really do not need.

Automobile Savings

Keep the clunker. In *Master Your Money* I said the cheapest car you will ever own is the one you presently own. This comment generated more discussion than just about anything else in the book—to the point where one friend suggested that the line be inscribed on my tombstone! The jokes may fly, but the fact is that, with the sticker prices and financing charges on today's new cars, you could spend about three thousand dollars per year to maintain your old vehicle and still come out ahead. Unless it is simply not safe to drive, hang on to your current car—and your cash.

Choose low-maintenance cars. If you must purchase a new car, research the market before you buy. Maintenance costs on different models of similar style cars can vary as much as 25 percent. Also, make your purchase at the end of the day or the end of the month, when quota-driven dealers are eager to close deals.

Comparison shop. If major repairs are needed on your car, get more than one estimate. Often the prices will vary by several hundred dollars. The same holds true for insurance policies; shop around to get the best price to meet your individual needs.

Clothing Costs

Read care labels. Be wary of "dry-clean only" items that can double or even triple the long-term cost of a garment.

Shop the outlets. Designer names have joined the ranks of veteran off-price retailers in offering clothing at 20 to 60 percent off department-store prices. Garage sales, too, offer unbeatable bargains—particularly on children's clothing, which is often "grown out" rather than "worn out."

Learn to sew. A girl's dress that sells for fifty or sixty dollars in a retail store can often be made for less than ten dollars. Fabric stores offer inexpensive lessons for beginners, and pattern manufacturers provide dozens of easy-to-sew garments that can be made in a matter of hours.

Education Expenses

Go public. Pick a highly rated public university over a private school and save twenty to sixty thousand dollars in four years.

Seek scholarships. Check with high school guidance counselors and local libraries to find scholarships that match your child's needs and talents. Funds ranging from twenty-five-dollar awards to full-tuition scholarships and grants are available for just about anyone willing to take the time to wade through the application process.

Ask your boss. Many companies have assistance programs designed to help employees fund their children's tuition.

Entertainment Options

Travel smart. Time your vacations to coincide with off-peak rates, when deals will be better and destinations less crowded. Discount travel consolidators and members-only travel clubs can also offer significant savings because they buy tickets and accommodations in bulk.

Plan ahead. Schedule an evening to dine in with friends, or plan to catch an early movie to avoid paying top dollar. Dine out on early-bird specials and use coupons or discount entertainment books to take advantage of meal deals.

Get creative. Learn a new sport or hobby. Check out a stack of library books to devour with a batch of home-baked cookies. Instead of spending forty dollars for tickets to a comedy club, get a group of friends together to play tennis or go bowling—and get a lot more laughs for your money.

The cost-cutting list could go on and on. Other ideas include buying generic brands, negotiating with salespeople to lower the price of an item, and stockpiling things like baby or birthday gifts that can be purchased out-of-season or on sale.

Check with your employer about matching programs that can markedly increase your savings potential. And again, shop around: Medical care, home furnishings, and even investments are all available at deeply discounted prices—if you are willing to do the research to locate the best buys for your particular needs.

LONG-TERM BENEFITS

Cutting costs and controlling spending will obviously have an immediate and positive effect on your cash-flow margin. Even better than this reward, though, are the long-term benefits of spending smart.

First and foremost, spending within your income will give you peace of mind—an invaluable commodity in an age of economic uncertainty. I remember the first time I ever budgeted for a vacation. The money had been set aside in advance, and we had no anxiety about overspending with credit cards. I think that was the first vacation I ever really enjoyed.

Another long-term benefit comes when you let the magic of compounding work for you. If you are in debt, compounding always works against you. If you save money, however, watch what happens: By saving, or underspending, $83 per month for forty years, you can accumulate $1,000 a year, totaling $40,000! Thanks to the magic of compounding, though, you can invest the $83 in an IRA earning 12½ percent and wind up with a million-dollar retirement fund. Even a 6 percent return would earn you about $500,000. Smaller still, with a savings account offering a meager 3 percent yield, you will still wind up with $250,000—and you only had to spend $40,000 to get it!

Thanks to compounding, a third long-term benefit of controlled spending is increased financial freedom. Of course, to get to this point you will probably have to delay gratification as you monitor spending along the way, but the ultimate liberty you gain makes it all well worth the wait.

And if you do not need the extra resources to live on in the future, you will have the potential to increase your giving, thereby "storing up treasures in heaven" and reaping eternal rewards.

A fifth, and significant, benefit of smart spending is the testimony, or example, you set for your children and your community. Anyone can force himself or herself to cough up a few bucks for the company's Christmas Cheer campaign. To share your resources on a regular basis, however, and with a joyful attitude, is both unique and noteworthy in today's self-serving, financially insecure society. With the help of the Holy Spirit and a healthy dose of savvy spending that is exactly the legacy you can create.

Finally, a lifestyle that relies on spending less than you earn will yield the reward of satisfaction in a job well done. Again, the discipline that smart spending requires may not come easy, but when it is done right, the long-term results certainly do feel good.

Marking Your Lifestyle "Finish Line"

As our national economy continues to stagger between recovery and recession, the fear of the future has inspired a reevaluation of financial priorities. Where salary, status, and acquisitions once reigned supreme as the measurements of success, the focus is now shifting to simpler, less pressure-filled lives. "No one," says one financial editor, "wants to be a slave to his money anymore."

For those who call themselves Christians, this reevaluation ought to come as a natural consequence of an identity that is rooted in Christ. If you need "things" to meet your needs, it will not be merely difficult to live within your income; it will be virtually impossible.

Establish some sort of a finish line on your lifestyle.

If, on the other hand, you look to Christ as your source of supply, then living within your income becomes simply a normal part of a fulfilled and purposeful life.

As a prerequisite to achieving this fulfillment, establish some sort of a finish line on your lifestyle. This end mark transcends the business of periodic goal setting such as we discussed in Chapter 5. Rather, this is a lifestyle measurement designed to answer the question, How much is enough?

One of our clients, Joe, is a young pediatrician. When he got out of medical school, he and his wife set limits on the kind of lifestyle they wanted to achieve; these limits applied to every area from housing to vacations. Sharing this vision with us, Joe asked that we develop a financial plan and hold him accountable for not exceeding his self-imposed limits.

As a result of his foresight and discipline, Joe has been able to give away more than half of his income many years. This giving was a cornerstone of his initial financial plan, yet to adhere to his commitment required more than just a generous spirit and a hefty salary. Joe had to learn to receive.

For example, Joe's in-laws invited him to bring his wife and children for a visit—a trip that required cross-country airfare. The trip had not been figured into their family budget, and Joe was afraid he would have to tell his in-laws they could not afford to come. But without his bringing it up, they offered to pay half the airfare for the entire family—a gift that Joe gratefully—and humbly—accepted.

A similar event occurred when Joe was making his rounds at the hospital. As he talked with a young patient, the child's father commented on the well-worn state of Joe's shoes. On his feet for the better part of his day, Joe figured he went through two to three pairs of shoes each year.

It turned out that the father was involved with a shoe-repair business, and he offered to resole Joe's shoes for free. Again, Joe thankfully accepted the offer, recognizing God's hand of provision in even something so seemingly trivial as a doctor's shoes.

Joe is not a cheapskate or a miser. He is a man who wants to give God all he possibly can, and he has disciplined himself and his family to live within the boundaries of their finish line—regardless of society's perspective on the situation. Because of his commitment, our firm estimates that Joe will ultimately give away ten times more than what he would have had he stuck strictly with the biblical guidelines of a 10 percent tithe.

One of the biggest reasons behind Joe's success is that he set his finish line early in his career. How much easier it is to commit to a lifestyle before you achieve it than to try to scale down once you become accustomed to a higher standard of living and allow luxuries to become necessities.

Unless you predetermine what you need and answer the question "How much is enough?" you will never reach a position of lasting peace and contentment. There will always be more things to buy, more vacations to take, a bigger house to aspire to, and a grander set of financial goals.

Unless you predetermine what you need and answer the question "How much is enough?" you will never reach a position of lasting peace and contentment.

If, on the other hand, you establish a realistic finish line for your lifestyle, you will realize lasting security, no matter what circumstances the future holds. By accepting the disciplines of money well spent, you will discover the blueprint for a life well spent.

Step 4:
Avoid the
Use of Debt

When I speak to Christian groups, I occasionally encounter people who say they are counting on the Rapture to get them out of debt. Usually, such comments are made with tongue firmly planted in cheek— although sometimes I suspect they reflect a genuine philosophy!

I like to point out Psalm 37:21: "The wicked borrows and does not repay." I often follow this reference with a question: "What if Jesus only raptures those who are debt-free?" This thought typically elicits a cough of nervous laughter from the crowd.

"You know," I then wonder aloud, "the Rapture may have already occurred!"

We often treat debt with similar jokes or a shoulder-shrugging attitude. Judging by the published material on this subject, however, we obviously get serious about it at some point. Today's books and articles spend more time dealing with debt than any other economic subject, with the possible exceptions of taxes and investments. I devoted a significant portion of *Master Your Money* to helping people conquer debt, and my book *Taming the Money Monster* tackles the subject from cover to cover.

Looking at the statistics, it is not hard to see why the discussion of debt generates so much interest. The average American family devotes fully 25 percent of its spendable income to outstanding debts! Indebtedness has become a pillar of our financial framework; life without any debt load is all but impossible to imagine.

We wink at debt—yet, in financially fragile times, indebtedness can imperil our survival. Think about it. Could you continue to meet your financial obligations— car payments, credit-card bills, installment loans, and the like—if you lost your job? What if an investment suddenly soured?

> **In financially fragile times, indebtedness can imperil our survival.**

In this chapter we will view debt through the window of economic uncertainty. We'll look for answers to questions such as: Is it ever okay to borrow money? How much debt can your financial structure support? These days, can anyone really afford a debt-free lifestyle? How do you get out of debt?

The answers will enable you to approach debt with a proper perspective. Debt does not have to threaten your economic comfort or survival. Debt may be a monster— but it is a beast you can tame.

WHAT DOES DEBT DO?

Today we tend to use terms such as *credit, borrow,* and *debt* almost interchangeably. There is, however, a significant distinction between the three. You have credit when someone gives you the right to borrow money.

When you exercise this right, you actually borrow the money. And, until you are able to repay your obligation, you are in debt.

Indebtedness is not something that seems to really bother today's buyers. The late Lewis Grizzard, the Atlanta newspaper columnist quoted in Chapter 4, admitted that he once bought an automobile that cost nearly six times what it had cost his mother and stepfather to build a new house in 1956. He said he financed the car, "of course." Another person, Mary, feels so proud whenever she whittles her credit-card balance down to around six or seven hundred dollars that she rewards herself—usually by charging a new designer dress. All told, our society has run up a whopping one-trillion-dollar tab in consumer debt . . . and the invitations continue: "Buy now and save! Make no payments until next March!"

Anytime you use credit to borrow money, you precommit your future income.

Yet borrowing money has its price—and it is a cost far greater than the low interest rates trumpeted by every lending institution in recent years. Anytime you use credit to borrow money, you precommit your future income. The effects of such obligations can range from simple inconvenience to financial devastation. Let's look at some of those consequences in more detail.

The Consequences of Debt

Money borrowed today must be repaid tomorrow. If you use credit to purchase an item now, counting on future income to make good on your promise to pay, you will inevitably encounter one, if not both, of the following consequences:

1. You will have reduced freedom in the future. Mentally, emotionally, and—especially—financially, you will not experience the comfort level you could have known had you not precommitted your resources. Opportunity will knock, but you may not be free to answer the door.

2. You will face built-in constraints on financial decisions you make today. Of course, every budget comes with ready-made restrictions based on individual spending and savings goals, but indebtedness only adds pickets to the fence. Like the proverbial monkey on your back, the money you owe will always be there to dictate your decisions and remind you of what you can—and cannot—do. Even if your income level rises, you will not be able to do as much with your money as you could were the funds not already earmarked for debt repayment.

If we want to prepare ourselves for an economically uncertain future, it stands to reason that we will want to operate from a position of emotional and financial freedom. Opportunities may present themselves in prosperous times, yet they seem to crop up faster than the weeds when times are tough—and we will want to take advantage of our options as we spot them.

Two principles to keep in mind as you work to strengthen your financial position reflect two sides of the same coin:

- Maximize your flexibility.
- Minimize your constraints.

As you aim to follow these maxims, an option that makes good sense from a strictly economic standpoint may not actually be a wise move. For example, one of my daughters lives in Nashville, Tennessee, where her husband is in graduate school. At one point just prior to the birth of their first child, they had an opportunity to purchase a condominium with monthly mortgage payments of $435—just $20 per month more than they were paying in rent on their one-bedroom apartment. They certainly needed the added space, and the property was selling below appraisal.

Economically, the purchase made sense—yet, as my daughter told me, they did not know how long they planned to stay in Nashville. Even though they could probably resell the condominium, they did not want to obligate themselves in any way that might limit their future options.

The Benefits of Debt-Free Living

If borrowing money limits financial flexibility, the absence of debt makes for a lifestyle of freedom and opportunity. With no, or even low, financial precommitments, you will be at liberty to pursue your goals and desires.

Not too long ago I spoke with a man who earned a hefty paycheck as a successful salesman. His desire, though, was to become involved in full-time Christian ministry. Having heard me speak on the benefits of debt-free living, he and his wife decided to pay off all their debts and start living within their income.

> **The absence of debt makes for a lifestyle of freedom and opportunity.**

Soon thereafter, the fellow realized his heart's desire when he accepted a position with Focus on the Family, which is where I met him. He told me that he and his wife now lived on a salary that was half of what he had made in sales—and yet, thanks to their lack of debt and controlled spending, they actually had more money and greater financial freedom than ever before!

For Christians, the freedom from the financial obligations of debt can spell all the difference in how effectively personal resources can be used by God. The IRS calculates that the average taxpayer—Christians included—spends more than ten times as much money paying off interest on debts as he or she gives to charitable causes!

The flip side of the money spent—or lost—on interest payments is the money that can be saved—or earned—through debt retirement. Getting rid of any debt—whether it is a large home mortgage or a relatively small credit-card balance—is a guaranteed profitable investment.

Getting rid of any debt is a guaranteed profitable investment.

For example, if you use credit cards to borrow two thousand dollars to finance Christmas purchases, an annual vacation, or even just run-of-the mill spending, you will incur an interest cost of around 18 percent. Should you opt to repay it by making only the seemingly easy minimum monthly payments, it will take you thirty-two years to do the job—and you will ultimately spend eight thousand dollars in interest, over and above the two-thousand-dollar principal!

If, on the other hand, you immediately repay the two thousand dollars, you will, from an investment standpoint, actually save eight thousand dollars. Still better off is the buyer who uses his or her own cash to make the purchases in the first place, escaping altogether the possibility of paying interest that is four times greater than the actual amount borrowed.

COMMON QUESTIONS AND CONCERNS

By now I hope I have convinced you to at least take a cautious and well-considered approach to borrowing. However, even the most conservative money handler is apt to face the possibility of debt at some point, and all of us have questions on the subject. In this section I want to answer some of the most commonly asked questions. And as we discuss these questions and answers, keep in mind that concerns that are entirely valid in the decisions of day-to-day living often take on a whole new significance when they are explored in light of economic uncertainty.

What causes debt?

Electronics shops are dangerous places for me. I walk in and immediately come upon a host of gadgets and equipment that I had not realized I needed until that moment. Bombarded by the sights and sounds of modern technology, I find myself filled with desire. With a billfold full of credit cards and salespersons promising things like "0 percent financing with no payments until February," buying becomes as easy as signing my name.

Concerns that are entirely valid in the decisions of day-to-day living often take on new significance when they are explored in light of economic uncertainty.

You may meet your temptations elsewhere: in dress shops, hardware stores, sporting-goods outlets, or other places. Whatever the store, unplanned purchases typically represent "impulse buys"—and more often than not they open the door to debt.

Debt can result from any number of factors, from poor planning to impatience to greed. Many people justify indebtedness with the thought that they are making an investment when they purchase items such as furniture, artwork, or even "dress-for-success" clothing. Others accept debt as a means of acquiring possessions to boost their self-image or "keep up with the Joneses."

Each of these causes, from poor planning to peer pressure, is a symptom of a deeper, root problem: a lack of reliance on the Holy Spirit's guidance and control.

> A Spirit-controlled person will enjoy a new life marked by "love, joy, peace, longsuffering, kindness, goodness, faithfulness, gentleness, [and] self-control."

A Spirit-controlled person will enjoy a life marked by "love, joy, peace, longsuffering [i.e., patience], kindness, goodness, faithfulness, gentleness, [and] self-control," as explained in Galatians 5:22–23. Each of these qualities can work to ward off debt: Patience, for example, allows you to wait on making a purchase you cannot currently afford; self-control offers protection against impulse buying; and peace contributes to a self-worth and an identity that are not dependent on possessions or the trappings of worldly success.

Living under the Holy Spirit's control runs against the grain of our credit-driven society. In fact, those who practice patience and self-control are often looked upon as tightwads, killjoys, or just plain misfits.

> Living under the Holy Spirit's control runs against the grain of our credit-driven society.

Indebtedness has become so common that we have convinced ourselves that borrowing is both necessary and right—regardless of the motivation. Yet when a financial decision is made out of envy or selfish ambition—as is sometimes the case when credit is used—the result, according to James 3:16, is "confusion and every evil thing."

There is only one solution to the temptations and pressures created by the almost universal embracing of credit in our society today. We must first pinpoint the cause of our desire to borrow money.

Are you wrestling with greed? Self-indulgence? A longing to present yourself to others on a certain materialistic level? Most importantly, are you experiencing fruits of the Spirit such as gentleness, joy, and peace—or do you sense the confusion indicative of jealousy or selfish ambition?

Having answered questions like these, you can trace the problem to its source: your identity in Christ. Until your identity is firmly rooted in Christ and His teachings, and until you live daily under the lordship and control of the Holy Spirit, you will never experience true freedom from the causes—and effects—of debt.

What about using credit to take advantage of opportunities?

I received a call from a friend in Dallas not too long ago. "I just got a chance to make a great investment—can I tell you about it?" he asked.

I listened—and it turned out that my friend wanted to buy a new luxury car that was priced below what he would normally expect to pay. He wanted to finance the purchase, reasoning that he could write off the 12 percent interest and earn another tax deduction as the automobile depreciated.

Why, I wondered, would anyone ever make an "investment" that was guaranteed to go down in value—and pay an additional 12 percent in interest to do it? I advised my friend to get to the root of his desire and admit that he had an "ego need" to drive a luxury car. I told him to go ahead and buy the car if he felt he had to—but to pay cash rather than use credit to make the purchase.

"Pay cash!" he exclaimed. "I can't afford that!"

My friend had fallen prey to a classic trap: He had succumbed to the illusion that he faced a fantastic opportunity. But just because the car was "on sale" did not mean it represented any sort of investment.

Salesmen and advertisers are experts at luring unwary shoppers with "Buy now!" campaigns that rely on the use of credit. Fearing that we may miss a "golden opportunity," we often buy things we cannot afford—and regret it later. As you confront such "opportunities" and "investments" in the future, remember the old saying: If it sounds too good to be true, it probably is.

Is it ever okay to borrow money?

Based on our discussion of debt up to this point, it may seem that borrowing is always a mistake. There are times, however, when using credit is both acceptable and even necessary.

> **Fearing that we may miss a "golden opportunity," we often buy things we cannot afford—and regret it later.**

Using credit can be a wise financial move. Imagine a family that needs shoes for the children. They do not have the money for shoes today, but they will within two weeks when Dad's paycheck comes. If there is a sale on the shoes they planned to purchase, using credit to acquire them at the cheaper price makes good sense—provided they do, in fact, make the funds from Dad's check available to pay off the credit-card balance.

I often use credit cards. Each time I charge a purchase, I deduct that amount from my checkbook. Then when the monthly bill arrives, I can easily write a check to repay the entire balance. Using this system, I may enjoy the convenience credit cards offer while avoiding any interest penalties. Also, by letting the credit-card company assume my obligations for a month while my own funds sit in an interest-earning checking account, I actually make money off the deal!

A home mortgage is one of the most common uses of credit that people point to as being justifiable or sensible. In times of appreciating real estate values or exceptionally low interest rates, I tend to agree: Buying a home does make good economic sense, even if you have to take out a loan to make the purchase.

In times of economic uncertainty, assuming such a large debt as a home mortgage may not be wise.

In times of economic uncertainty, however, assuming such a large debt may not be wise. Can you, as a homeowner, handle the stress associated with a plateau—or worse, a drop—in the value of your home? Can you continue to make monthly payments if you do not receive an expected pay raise?

The main question you must ask yourself before buying a home is, "How much economic uncertainty or upheaval do I expect to see?" If, for example, you are convinced that an all-out financial collapse is just around the corner, you should not make the purchase. If your judgment is correct and some type of collapse does occur, home prices will almost certainly fall. Having waited, you will be in a position to take advantage of what will likely be an underpriced, oversupplied real estate market.

Less mortgage is always better than more mortgage, no matter how long you plan to stay in the home.

If, on the other hand, you decide that any coming economic downswings will not be too severe or crippling, you may feel comfortable in taking the home-ownership plunge. If you do, I suggest you make as large a down payment as possible and assume the shortest-term mortgage you can afford. Less mortgage is always better than more mortgage, no matter how long you plan to stay in the home.

Whether you contemplate taking on debt to pay for a home, send a child to college, take a family vacation, or just make a few credit-card purchases, several principles should always govern your decisions:

- The decision to borrow money must make good economic sense. The economic return must be greater than the economic cost.

Check your motives before going into debt.

- The decision must not create undue stress. The greater the debt, the greater the stress; how much stress can you—or your marriage—handle?

- The decision must be one in which you have genuine freedom from God. Colossians 3:15 says, "Let the peace of God rule in your hearts." Check your motives before going into debt. Are you rushing into an uncertain financial commitment? Or has God given you the go-ahead through peace?

These criteria represent wise guidelines for using credit, yet there are also certain situations that may trigger the need for debt simply because there is no other alternative. What parent, for example, would refuse to use a credit card to check a sick or injured child into a hospital's emergency room? In a situation such as that, payments would be justified at any cost.

Likewise, accident victims, abandoned spouses, flood-ravaged farmers, and others may find themselves unable to survive without incurring debt to some degree. Before assuming this kind of obligation, however, you must ask yourself whether or not your goals can be met in any other way. Taking on debt should be viewed as a last resort for use in extreme situations. You must be sure your need fits this bill.

If going into debt really is the only solution to your particular problem, you must first establish some sort of repayment plan. Without that, it becomes easy to borrow—and burrow—your way deeper and deeper into trouble.

Getting out of debt is always harder than getting in.

How do I get out of debt?

Whether your debt is due to unwise overspending or an unexpected calamity, one thing is certain: Getting out of debt is always harder than getting in.

It is much easier to borrow money than it is to repay it—especially when the thing you used the money for has already been consumed. If you borrow to buy a home, at least you can enjoy living in it; however, if you use a credit card to charge an expensive dinner at a posh restaurant, chances are you will not have such a healthy appetite when you get the bill the following month.

Getting out of debt may be hard, but it is never impossible.

Getting out of debt may be hard, but it is never impossible. Ken was only in his early thirties, and he had already accumulated debts in excess of $50,000, plus his home mortgage. He had two car payments, and ten totally maxed-out credit cards.

The financial strain took its toll on Ken's marriage, and it collapsed. With two households to maintain, creditors calling daily, and no means to repay his debts, Ken found himself on the brink of financial and emotional ruin.

Happily, Ken did not fall victim to panic or paralysis. He took responsibility for his situation and began a proactive strategy to get debt-free.

The only way to conquer debt is to cut your spending, and that's what Ken did. He sold his home and moved into a small apartment. Next, he took a financial physical, scrutinizing his position and examining his spending patterns. Finally, he set a goal of saving seventy dollars per month to pay off his debts.

To make his plan work, Ken evaluated any potential purchases with these questions: Do I really need this? Can I get by with less? Am I paying too much?

He got creative, canceling magazine subscriptions and cable television service and foregoing things like movies in favor of less costly entertainment such as reading and exercise. It took four years and a healthy dose of discipline, but Ken is now totally debt-free.

Ken's story illustrates both the burden of debt and the path to financial freedom. A lot of people wish there were some systematic, magical, or easy way out of debt. The fact of the matter is, however, that the only answer is to decrease your spending, increase your income, get an inheritance, or strike oil in your backyard. Of these, the only truly workable and immediate alternative is to cut spending.

Before you break out the scissors in a frenzy of random cost-cutting measures, though, take a moment to evaluate your situation according to the following strategy:

1. Be honest about what caused the debt, then deal with the root problem. Fixing your identity in Christ and developing the right perspective on debt (as will be outlined in the conclusion of this chapter) will help you conquer problems such as greed or a poor self-image.

2. Be honest with where you are in terms of the

total amount of your debt. Like Ken, you need to add up all of your obligations—from mortgage and car payments to credit-card balances and overdue bills.

3. **Establish a realistic repayment plan and discipline yourself to follow it.** Ken began by saving just seventy dollars per month, and he paid off the smallest bills first to give himself encouragement. Do not kid yourself or overestimate your ability to repay.

There is no quick or painless way to get rid of debt.

Consider your individual temperament: Do you need to be held accountable to someone? Do you work best with the motivation of some promised reward?

Beware of overambition. Like the would-be dieter who starves himself for three days and then ravenously plunges headlong into a pan of lasagna, financial "diets" that are too severe or demanding can come to a speedy ruin. And if you encounter failure in the early steps of any campaign, getting restarted may seem like an impossible chore.

I am occasionally asked if people should continue to tithe while working to pay off their debts. I say absolutely yes—unless you reveal your entire financial position to your pastor and he agrees that you should stop giving for a time. In this case, you must hold yourself accountable to someone who has the wisdom to monitor your financial moves.

Establishing and following a realistic repayment plan is critical to the success of your debt-retirement strategy. Again, there is no quick or painless way to get rid of debt, but by using this Debt Repayment worksheet you can chart a course toward financial freedom. Once your strategy is in place, all you will need is the self-discipline to make it work.

Debt Repayment Worksheet

Date: _____

DEBTS	Amount Due Monthly
1. Home mortgage	
2. Credit-card balances due	
Visa	
MasterCard	
Department store	
Other	
3. Car payments	
4. Student loans	
5. Credit union loans	
6. Business borrowing	
7. Amount owed to friends or relatives	
8. Other	
9. **Total monthly outflow needed for debt repayment** (Add lines 1 through 8)	
INCOME SOURCES	**Amount Received**
10. Available income from normal sources (see "Cash-flow margin" on the Cash Flow Analysis worksheet in Chapter 6)	
11. Additional income from odd jobs	
12. Income available after reduced spending	
13. Income from sale of assets	
14. Gifts from relatives and friends	
15. Other income	
16. **Total monthly income available for debt repayment** (add lines 10 through 15)	

Subtract your total monthly debt obligations from your total monthly available income (line 16 minus line 9). If the final amount is a negative number, you will need to be creative in coming up with ways to further increase your income and reduce your spending. Discipline your-self to apply any available margin—any excess cash—to-ward debt retirement.

WHAT DOES GOD THINK ABOUT DEBT?

Having read this far, you will not be surprised to learn that the Bible discourages debt. While borrowing is not expressly forbidden in Scripture, it is repeatedly warned against, particularly in Proverbs, God's how-to book on wise living.

"The borrower is servant to the lender," cautions Prov-erbs 22:7. Likewise, cosigning another's loan is risky busi-ness, according to verses 26 and 27: "Do not be one of those who shakes hands in a pledge, / One of those who is surety for debts; / If you have nothing with which to pay, / Why should he take away your bed from under you?"

I mentioned earlier in this chapter that "the wicked borrows and does not repay." Repayment of debt is a must from God's perspective—and as Proverbs 3:28 advises, the quicker the better. "Do not say to your neighbor, / 'Go, and come back, / And tomorrow I will give it,' / When you have it with you."

Why is God so opposed to debt? This attitude is hard medicine to take, given the financial mainstay that bor-rowing has become in our society today. One obvious rea-son is the bondage that comes with debt, both financially and emotionally. If our resources are precommitted be-cause of past credit use, we cannot be financially free to give as God directs us. Moreover, we may not even feel able to seek God's direction in our lives because even our physical movements may be restricted by our lack of disposable funds.

The Bible also discourages debt because it presumes upon the future—and on God. If you are concerned about economic uncertainty, the last thing you want to do is to take anything about the future for granted. You would not, for example, take on a new or bigger mortgage if you knew your company was about to go out of business. Likewise, if you knew the stock market was going to crash within three months, you would not invest any money today.

> **The Bible discourages debt because it presumes upon the future—and on God.**

If the financial forecast calls for difficult times ahead, you should work to get rid of all debt. To do otherwise is to presume upon the future—and violate the principles outlined in passages such as James 4:13–15: "Come now, you who say, 'Today or tomorrow we will go to such and such a city, spend a year there, buy and sell, and make a profit'; whereas you do not know what will happen tomorrow. For what is your life? It is even a vapor that appears for a little time and then vanishes away. Instead you ought to say, 'If the Lord wills, we shall live and do this or that.'"

And the Lord's will often becomes clear through financial restrictions. Could it be that if you cannot afford something, God does not want you to have it? Or perhaps God is telling you to wait. I know of a missionary family who felt frustrated because they lacked the necessary funds to begin working in Russia—only to later learn that God had held them back because their talents were needed much more in another country. Had they been able to borrow the money to do what they thought God wanted them to do, they would have made a mistake. By borrowing, many people get ahead of God and wind up doing things He never intended them to do!

Remember, God promises to supply all of our needs (Matt. 6:25–34). He says nothing, however, about giving in to our greed, impatience, or peer-pressure-induced longings. He cannot be counted on to get us out of a financial hole we have thoughtlessly dug for ourselves.

By borrowing, many people get ahead of God and wind up doing things He never intended them to do!

Living Together in Unity

For married couples, many of these financial holes may be avoided by adhering to one of marriage's built-in safeguards: namely, the differing perspectives that husbands and wives have on financial matters.

I believe God puts men and women together to complement and complete one another. Psalm 133:1 says, "How good and how pleasant it is / For brethren to dwell together in unity!" Applying this principle to marriage and money, I submit that borrowing decisions should never be made without the full consent of both spouses.

Every year couples seeking advice on a potential investment tell me about hundreds of "great deals." In almost every case, the deal promoter is the husband. The wife is typically more reserved, being far less willing to risk losing their capital than her scheme-happy or entrepreneurial husband.

Borrowing decisions should never be made without the full consent of both spouses.

When I speak to men on this subject, I urge them to follow two rules:

- If you cannot explain an investment or a need for debt to your wife so she can understand it, you do not understand the situation well enough to make the investment or incur the debt.

- If you can and do explain a potential financial move to your wife and she does not feel good about it, do not pursue it.

I spent years failing to apply these two rules in my communication with Judy. As a result, I missed the counsel of a very wise person. Like many men, I assumed that because my wife was not a CPA and had no formal training in finance or economics she could not understand all of our financial circumstances. The truth is, women often have an intuitive sense that men lack—especially concerning money matters and debt, in particular. Wisdom does not always require intellectual understanding. Consider the example of Abigail, whose story is told in 1 Samuel 25.

Wisdom does not always require intellectual understanding.

Abigail and her husband Nabal made an interesting pair. She was beautiful and intelligent; he was surly, wicked, and foolish. Nabal was also very wealthy. His holdings included a thousand goats and three thousand sheep.

David and his men had protected Nabal's shepherds as they went about their work. At sheepshearing time, David sent messengers to ask Nabal for some sort of hospitality in return. Scoffing at the request, Nabal refused. When David heard Nabal's response, he mounted an attack, intending to kill Nabal and all of his men.

Abigail learned what had happened and she immediately set about straightening things out. Packing a feast for six hundred men, she rode out to meet David's war party. She humbly begged David's pardon, acknowledged his destiny as leader over Israel, and advised him to avoid vindictiveness. Blessing Abigail for her good judgment, David dismissed her in peace.

Abigail probably knew little about Nabal's business dealings, and she certainly did not share David's experience as a warrior. Yet, thanks to her sensible actions and wise words, she protected both men. She saved Nabal's life, and in doing so, she kept David from bloodying his hands in improper vengeance.

Like many women, Abigail did not need intellectual understanding or personal experience to make a smart move. She instinctively knew what to say and do. David recognized this and benefited greatly from her advice. Nabal, on the other hand, did not even consider discussing the matter with his wife. And when he finally did grasp the significance of what had happened, he had some sort of heart attack and died.

> **Choosing to follow rules about debt will probably mean you cannot have everything you want whenever you want it.**

I want to challenge men to be like David instead of Nabal. When I began discussing our finances with Judy and listening to her advice, I noticed a dramatic improvement in the quality and wisdom of our decisions. Where I once felt defensive or insecure when faced with her questions, I now realize that they offer the perfect opportunity to discover just how well I understand—and can explain—a potential financial move.

The need for spousal unity is just one of the principles God offers to enable us to use credit wisely. Other safeguards are all around us, from biblical references on borrowing to the seemingly limitless battery of books written on the subject. We must learn and apply the regulations for dealing with debt. Of course, choosing to follow such rules will probably mean you cannot have everything you want whenever you want it. What you will have, though, is a better treasure by far: the peace of mind that comes from knowing you are on the right path—regardless of what the future brings.

Throughout this book I have urged you to think and act responsibly to follow Scripture's time-tested principles for taking charge of your finances. As we face economic uncertainty, the question of who—or what—is in control of your resources takes on a supreme significance.

If you are saddled with debt, your finances will control you. On the other hand, if you practice wise steward-ship and remain unhindered by debt's bondage, you will be in control—and you will be free to look to the Lord to supply guidance, direction, and peace, regardless of the uncontrolled and uncontrollable economic future of our nation and world.

8

Step 5:
Increase
Your Giving

Henry is a terrific salesman. He is also a Christian. For several years, he raked in about one hundred thousand dollars annually and dutifully earmarked 10 percent—or ten thousand dollars—for tithing.

One year, though, Henry outdid himself and brought home close to three hundred thousand dollars. Faced with a tax problem at the year's end, he sought the advice of one of our financial planners.

"What do you want to do in terms of your year-end giving?" the planner asked.

Henry explained how he had already given his normal ten thousand dollars—which, he figured, pretty much covered him in terms of a tithe.

"No," countered the planner, "the tithe on three hundred thousand dollars is thirty thousand dollars. To meet that, you'd have to give away twenty thousand dollars more."

Taken aback, Henry protested that there was no way he could write a check for twenty thousand dollars. "God wouldn't expect that!" he reasoned. "He knows I've given already—this is just an unusual year."

The financial planner paused for a moment, then quietly asked a question. "Where," he said, "do you think the three hundred thousand dollars came from?"

While most of us do not have three hundred thousand dollars to tithe from, we do share Henry's reluctance to part with "our" hard-earned money. Yet that is exactly what God asks us to do. The Bible never applauds an accumulator; time and again, God's praise is reserved for the giver.

> **The Bible never applauds an accumulator; time and again, God's praise is reserved for the giver.**

On one occasion Christ met a young man who wanted to know the secret to eternal life. The fellow had led a good, clean life, keeping all of the commandments—yet he knew he still lacked something.

Jesus advised the man to sell all that he had and give the proceeds to the poor. Disheartened, the fellow "went away sorrowful, for he had great possessions" (Matt. 19:22).

Why was Christ so eager to separate the young man from his money? Was He holding out the promise of heaven like a carrot, as the ultimate fund-raising gimmick?

> **Will you control your money, or will it control you?**

No. Jesus knew the young man was wealthy—and that he had placed his trust in his own wallet. Until he could bring himself to part with that financial security blanket, the rich young man would never be free to place his trust in Christ. He would never know the true riches and security of eternal life.

Like the rich young man, you have a choice to make. Will you control your money, or will it control you? Our tendency, particularly during financially trying times, is to want to hang on to what we have. As we do that, though, we transfer our trust further and further away from God and deeper and deeper into our own inadequate resources.

Henry's story has a happy ending. The day after their meeting, the financial planner got a call from Henry's wife. "My husband was awake all night wrestling with your question, 'Where did the money come from?'" she said. "Eventually, he got out of bed and wrote a twenty-thousand-dollar check. Then, and only then, did he finally feel free and at peace."

> **Financial freedom begins with a willingness to give.**

Financial freedom begins with a willingness to give. Henry recognized this principle, and in making his resources available to God, he received a liberating reward. This advantage is readily available to each one of us—once we discover exactly why, and how, we should give.

A PORTRAIT OF PRIORITIES

Henry's story is one that repeats itself every year on tax returns across the country. We may think the more money we make, the less trouble we will have tithing—but IRS statistics prove otherwise. As our salaries grow, our giving percentage does not keep pace. For example, as figure 8.1 shows, someone who makes a half million dollars per year gives away only 2.5 percent—no more than the person whose annual income is only twenty-five thousand dollars.

An even more sobering indictment may be leveled at American Christians. According to the National Association of Evangelicals, evangelical Christians gave away an average of 6.83 percent of their incomes in 1968. Twenty years later their salaries had grown fivefold—yet giving levels sank to only 4.73 percent.

1991 Giving Results

Income:	Average Gift	% of Income Given
Under $10,000	$ 239	3.6%
$10–19,999	507	3.4%
$20–29,999	617	2.5%
$30–39,999	640	1.8%
$40–49,999	1,038	2.3%
$50–74,999	1,230	2.0%
$75–99,999	1,666	1.9%
$100,000 and above	2,450	2.5%

Source: Independent Sector

Figure 8.1

Recognizing how many Christians fall short of the 10 percent mark mandated in the Old Testament, one pastor I know challenged his congregation with Malachi 3:8–10. This passage indicates that to tamper with or withhold even a portion of the tithe is to steal from God. "How many of you," the pastor asked, "drive stolen cars? Live in stolen houses? Wear stolen clothes?"

Some may balk or take offense at the implied accusations of such pointed questions. Yet when you consider our total spending habits, a mild surprise over our charitable shortcomings gives way to astonishment or dismay. Figure 8.2 contrasts our missions giving with selected consumer expenditures.

Statistics such as these paint an ugly portrait of our priorities. As American churchgoers, we are not even meeting the tithe—let alone giving sacrificially! Yet because the picture is one of a "faceless," corporate America, the

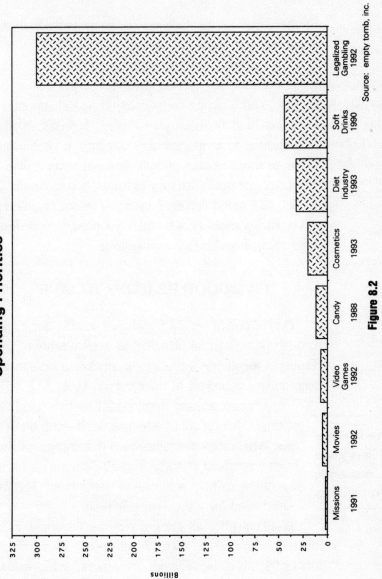

Spending Priorities

Billions

Missions 1991 · Movies 1992 · Video Games 1992 · Candy 1988 · Cosmetics 1993 · Diet Industry 1993 · Soft Drinks 1990 · Legalized Gambling 1992

Source: empty tomb, inc.

Figure 8.2

numbers may fail to challenge us, on an individual level, to reorient our individual spending priorities.

Giving should not be merely a pillar in your financial plan; it should be the cornerstone.

The money-management objectives we have considered so far—setting goals, following a spending plan, and avoiding debt—come as logical supports in a well-built financial plan. Giving, however, is often relegated to a discretionary category. It becomes no more than a noble pursuit that can nevertheless be postponed until such time as funds "become available." Yet, as I noted earlier, financial freedom begins with giving. Giving should not be merely a pillar in your financial plan; it should be the cornerstone.

FIVE GOOD REASONS TO GIVE

One of our firm's chief goals is to enable our clients, through wise financial planning, to free up more of their resources for giving. I want to encourage people to give generously—regardless of their income level.

There is never any good economic reason to give.

As our company developed, I spent a good deal of time thinking about why people do—and do not— give. What motivates a giver? Is it the strength of some heart-wrenching financial appeal? Genuine altruism— the desire to help someone or something? The perceived need for a tax write-off? Guilt?

People give for all sorts of reasons. For some, giving meets an ego need as their names appear on impressive lists of friends or benefactors. For others, giving—usually some token amount—is merely a way to avoid or lessen the nuisance of fund-raising appeals. Whatever the motivation, though, one fact is clear: There is never any good economic reason to give.

Financially speaking, giving does not make sense. When you give money away, you always have less of it for yourself. Even the much-ballyhooed tax breaks for charitable contributions do not keep pace with the size of the gifts themselves. Any donation—no matter how large or how small—reduces your total net worth.

So why do I want you to make giving part of your financial plan? I can think of at least five good reasons, every one of which will contribute to your ultimate financial freedom:

1. Giving Breaks the Power of Money

In times of economic uncertainty, the only people who seem to be free of financial worry are the naive, the uninformed, and the givers.

The naive simply do not have a clue as to the severity or urgency of their situation. "Don't confuse me with the facts," they seem to protest. Like Scarlett O'Hara in *Gone with the Wind,* they prefer not to concern themselves with potentially difficult circumstances, reasoning that they can "worry about that tomorrow."

The uninformed may be essentially perceptive people, yet they simply do not have the necessary facts to come to any educated conclusions. Ignorant about matters such as the national debt or tax rates, they fail to grasp the total financial picture and operate from a false sense of security.

The givers, on the other hand, understand the economic causes of fear—yet, because they have a biblical perspective on money, they experience real security and freedom. They have learned, firsthand, the truth of Matthew 6:8, that "your Father knows the things you have need of before you ask Him." Their trust in God's provision allows them to give with an open hand.

The world's perspective—that accumulation should be our ultimate goal—creates a bondage to money. "Get all you can, can all you get—and save the cans," advise modern pundits. Under this philosophy, any thought of giving money away comes as a threat to our overall security—and thus, we simply cannot give freely. We become slaves to our finances.

Givers, on the other hand, master their money. In giving their resources away, they relinquish worldly security and significance—acknowledging their dependence on and service to God. Money no longer has any hold on them.

Givers master their money.

Either we control our money, or it controls us. We cannot be accumulators first and still serve God. Luke 16:13 explains why this is so: "No servant can serve two masters; for either he will hate the one and love the other, or else he will be loyal to the one and despise the other. You cannot serve God and mammon."

2. Giving Promises Rewards

Again and again throughout Scripture, God's command to give goes hand-in-hand with a promise. "Honor the LORD with your possessions, . . . so your barns will be filled with plenty" (Prov. 3:9–10). "Bring all the tithes into the storehouse, . . . [and] you will be a delightful land" (Mal. 3:10–12). "Give, and it will be given to you" (Luke 6:38).

God is serious about giving. He knows—and He promises—that we will be better off for it.

Many people interpret this promise to mean that the

more they give, the more they will get. Were this actually the case, giving would become the hottest investment strategy on Wall Street. It would make unquestionably good economic sense.

The truth is that God's promised rewards are, I believe, much more significant than financial blessing. Material reward may—and often does—follow a faithful giver, yet it must be neither promised nor expected.

Instead, expect God to bless you in ways you may never have imagined. Perhaps He will give you good health, favor with your boss, or wisdom in your financial decision making. He may use your gift chiefly to draw you closer to Himself. He may, in fact, choose to bless you with an eternal reward—one that you will never see on this side of heaven. Whatever the case, give cheerfully. Your promised reward will surely come.

3. Giving Provides an Eternal Perspective

I have a friend who says his net worth is not the sum total that appears on his bank or accounting statements. Instead, he says his net worth is based on his faithfulness and generosity in giving. Because of his convictions, this fellow gives away 70 percent of his income every year. His basic needs are met, he enjoys complete financial freedom, and he sees his giving as an eternal—rather than temporal—investment.

The apostle Paul would have loved my friend. In Philippians 4:17, Paul commended the church members for their generosity toward him—not because of his needs, but because of the gifts that would be credited to their account. Paul was talking about the Philippians' eternal account—the place where, as Christ put it, "neither moth nor rust destroys and where thieves do not break in and steal" (Matt. 6:20).

Few people have articulated the importance of maintaining an eternal perspective better than the missionary Jim Elliot. I refer to his story often. Jim and his wife Elisabeth went to South America during the 1950s to work with the Auca Indians. Jim and four other men took a small airplane into the jungle to meet the tribe. They landed and were immediately murdered by Auca headhunters.

When Elisabeth received word that her husband had been martyred she resolved to stay in South America and live among the Indians, sharing with them the message of Jesus Christ.

> If you are truly concerned about economic uncertainty, it only makes sense to pursue that which is both certain and secure.

Today, nearly thirty years after Jim's death, many in the Auca tribe have become Christians. How did Elisabeth find the strength to see their mission through? How was she able to respond to the uncertain future with such courage and faith? A key to her resolve may be found in her husband's letters and journals: "He is no fool," Jim wrote, "who gives up what he cannot keep in order to gain what he cannot lose."

If you apply Jim's message in your financial life, and if you really believe in eternal rewards, why would you not want to give up something you cannot keep to get something you cannot lose? Why would you hang on to your money when you could have an eternal reward instead? After all, as the saying goes, "you can't take it with you." If you are truly concerned about economic uncertainty, it only makes sense to pursue that which is both certain and secure. It only makes sense to give.

4. Giving Demonstrates God's Ownership

God owns it all. If I could only proclaim one message, this would be it: Everything we have belongs to God. When we give, all we are really doing is demonstrating this fact.

Recognizing God's ownership of our resources—of all resources—is probably the single biggest key to financial freedom. Sally is a young mother I know. Not long ago she lost twenty dollars—a bill she had hurriedly thrust into her pocketbook as she dashed out the door for a quick trip to the grocery store before she was due to pick up a car pool of five preschoolers. She discovered the loss when she started to pay for her groceries and realized the money was gone.

Looking for a sympathetic ear, Sally later confided her trouble to the car pool. "Children," she sighed, "I just lost twenty dollars, and I'm feeling sad."

The questions and advice came rapid fire:

"What did you need the money for?"

"Can't you just go to the bank and get some more?"

"Maybe, if you ask her, my mommy will give you some of her money."

Sally could not help but smile at the youngsters' eagerness to help—and suddenly, her spirits lifted.

"You know what?" she said to herself as much as to the children, "God owns everything. He can help me find that money, or He can provide for us in some other way. We don't need to even worry about it!"

Thus liberated, Sally cheerfully finished her car pool rounds and drove home with a newfound peace and sense of security. She knew God would take care of her, and as she pulled into her driveway, she saw it. Tucked among the blanket of fall leaves that covered her drive was a twenty-dollar bill.

In acknowledging God's ownership of her resources, Sally was able to mentally release the twenty dollars and experience true freedom from worry. In so doing, she learned a valuable lesson about financial security: Financial freedom does not come with having money in your wallet when you go through the grocery-store checkout line. Financial freedom comes when you turn your resources fully over to God.

> **Financial freedom comes when you turn your resources fully over to God.**

When you manage your money with the conviction that it is actually God's money, giving becomes a logical, natural part of your total financial plan. It confirms God's ownership of your resources—demonstrating, again, that He really does "own it all."

5. Giving Demonstrates Obedience to God's Commands

How do you show your love for God? There are many ways to answer this question, but Jesus summed it up for us in John 14:15. "If you love Me," He said, "keep My commandments."

So just what does the Lord command when it comes to giving? In the Old Testament, a tithe was 10 percent—the first 10 percent—of any livestock, produce, or other sources of income. We have already discussed Malachi 3:8–10, in which God promised a curse for those who withhold the tithe and great blessings for those who give wholeheartedly. Likewise, the promise in Proverbs 3:9–10 is that if we honor the Lord with our wealth, with the "firstfruits" of all our crops, our "barns will be filled with plenty" and our "vats will overflow with new wine."

Today I am often asked whether we are supposed to tithe off of our gross paycheck or wait until the taxes and other withholdings have been taken out and then tithe off of what we actually receive, the net. My answer is simple: Do you want God to bless the gross or the net? God gives us the gross; therefore, we must tithe on the gross.

The net-versus-gross question loses much of its relevance when we examine the New Testament perspective on giving.

This net-versus-gross question loses much of its relevance, however, when we examine the New Testament perspective on giving. In 1 Corinthians 16:2, Paul admonishes the Christian to give "as he may prosper." We are to give as God has prospered us.

Also, our gifts should be generous because, as Christ tells us in Luke 6:38, we get what we give: "Give, and it will be given to you: good measure, pressed down, shaken together, and running over will be put into your bosom. For with the measure that you use, it will be measured back to you."

One danger in sticking too closely to the Old Testament specifics is that our perspective may get skewed. If we give only 10 percent again and again out of every paycheck, we may begin to feel that 10 percent is God's while the remaining 90 percent belongs to us. Remember: God owns it all.

The secret to giving generously is deciding, in advance, how much you really need to live on.

The secret to giving generously is deciding, in advance, how much money you really need to live on. Remember the pediatrician in Chapter 6? He set lifestyle goals early on, and as he reached them, he was able to give away all of the extra. Because of this commitment, the doctor will ultimately wind up giving away more than ten times what he would have had he toed the line on the 10 percent mark.

Plan to give. One of the biggest barriers to giving is that we wait until needs are presented to us and then we react to them. At that point, the money is rarely available—and no matter how much we may want to help, we are simply unable to do so.

THE PRICE OF FREEDOM

With so many Scriptures and practical reasons that mandate giving, why do we find it so difficult to put tithing at the top of our financial priority list? One answer is that we are afraid—particularly during times of economic uncertainty—to let even a few dollars out of our sight.

Frank is a man who, despite his considerable wealth, lives a very modest lifestyle. He has one grown child, a decent, average-sized home, and few material needs. He is a nice-enough guy—not the type to be considered cheap or miserly—yet he feels completely unable to give away even 1 percent of his income.

Frank grew up in poverty. He worked his way through school, and when he began to make money, he stewarded every dollar with care. Even when he had socked away several million dollars in liquid investments, he never purchased a large home or spent money unnecessarily.

Frank has a lot of money—yet he has no financial freedom. He is driven by fear, and his security rests chiefly in the presumed safety of a fat bankroll.

Another story concerns a woman I will call Jane. When her husband died, Jane lost everything. The man had had no life insurance, and without his income, Jane had no real means of providing for herself and her young son. Living in abject poverty and with only a bit of flour and some oil in her cupboard, she fully expected to starve to death.

One day Jane met a stranger who asked her for a piece of bread. Too desperate to hide behind a mask of pride, Jane explained her situation.

To her surprise, the man pressed on: "Don't be afraid," he said. "Just go home, make some bread, and bring it to me. You will not run out of food for your family."

Jane did what the stranger asked. She fixed a meal for him—that day and every day thereafter. And just as he had promised, her cupboards never were bare.

Jane is the widow whose story is chronicled in 1 Kings 17. The stranger is Elijah, the "man of God." By giving her meager resources away to Elijah, the widow experienced freedom and blessing unlike anything she had ever known. She no longer worried about having to buy food—and as a result, she won a genuine freedom from fear.

If your security is in Christ, you will be free to give—and in fact, you will want to give.

Given the choice, who would you rather be? Wealthy Frank, a slave to insecurity and fear—or Jane, who enjoyed total peace, security, and freedom as she placed all she had in God's hands? The difference between the two has nothing to do with the size of their bank accounts. Rather, the chief distinction lies in Frank and Jane's individual responses to God's command that we give.

Like Frank, many of our firm's clients have experienced worldly wealth—yet, because their security is in Christ and not in their resources, they are free to give as God commands. On average, in fact, they give away about 15 percent of their annual income—a marked contrast to the 2 to 4 percent levels of most Americans.

If your security is in Christ, you will be free to give—

and in fact, you will want to give. You do not, however, have to take my word on this. Scripture is full of illustrations and guidelines on giving. God Himself challenges us to discover the freedom and security that come with giving: "'Try Me now in this,' says the LORD of hosts, 'if I will not open for you the windows of heaven and pour out for you such blessing that there will not be room enough to receive it'" (Mal. 3:10).

God wants to give us financial freedom. He knows it does not come as a result of accumulation, no matter what our income level is. Placing your trust in material possessions and financial gain can only lead to bondage. You will be controlled by your money.

God asks us to give because He knows that is the only route to true financial freedom. By trusting in Christ and giving as the Lord commands, you will build a security system that cannot be penetrated by decay, thievery, fear, or even death. Your security will be eternal, bringing freedom both on earth and in heaven.

God wants to give us financial freedom.

PART
THREE

INVESTING IN
UNCERTAIN
ECONOMIC TIMES

9

Step 6:
Develop Your
Investment
Strategy

John Templeton is one of our generation's most success-ful long-term investors. After spending half a century as a professional, worldwide investment counselor, he noted that the secret to smart money management boiled down to one basic thing: common sense.

When you build something you want to keep, com-mon sense dictates that you build it according to a plan and with materials that will last. This strategy works for all types of construction, from putting together a financial portfolio to building a house. The television images of the devastating fires that swept through southern California during the summer of 1993 are pictures I will never forget. Some twenty-five thousand people lost their homes. Amid the charred ruins on a Laguna Beach hillside, though, there was one house the blaze had been unable to destroy.

Smart money management boils down to one basic thing: common sense.

That house belonged to a man named To Bui, a Viet-namese engineer. To Bui knew, firsthand, the dangers fire held; as an eight-year-old, he had watched his family's apartment burn to the ground. When he built his Califor-

nia home—in an area known for its susceptibility to fire—
To Bui invested a good deal of time and money to build
with fireproof materials.

To his neighbors living in their wood-shingle
homes, To Bui's red concrete-tile roof, thick stucco
walls, and double-paned windows must have looked
ridiculously expensive. When the fires came, though,
To Bui's foresighted wisdom was apparent. As others'
homes fell all around him, To Bui stood hosing down
his house with water to keep it cool.

> **The purpose of investing is to preserve the wealth you have accumulated through working and saving.**

In hindsight, To Bui's survival reflects his willingness to exercise common sense. He knew fire posed a
potential threat—and so did his neighbors. The difference
was in how they approached that risk.

Like To Bui's neighbors, many of today's investors
build their financial houses without a sensible plan. The
purpose of investing is to preserve the wealth you have
accumulated through working and saving. If you want to
protect your resources so that they will be available for
you and your children, you need a secure storm shelter.

In this chapter I want to help you develop a commonsense investment strategy. With this plan, you can weather
the economic storms of today as well as those in the far-off
financial future. In times of economic uncertainty, the
strength of your storm shelter—supported by your investment philosophy—will determine whether you struggle,
thrive, or just survive.

YOUR INVESTMENT PHILOSOPHY: TRUTH OR MYTHCONCEPTION?

Many investors believe that good decision making requires expert knowledge and constant updates. In reality,

though, the best decision makers are those who have developed a sound investment philosophy on which to base their choices.

As we counsel clients, our firm has identified two distinct investment philosophies. One is rooted in a secular perspective that is shaped by worldly "mythconceptions." The other is based on strategic truths that are outlined in the Bible and proven through practical experience. Consider the following contrasts:

- Secular Mythconception: Spend and consume, saving can wait.
- Strategic Truth: Save and invest, spending can wait.

As a society, Americans have run up a one-trillion-dollar tab in consumer debt. When buying opportunities present themselves, we take the bait, reasoning that there will always be money to save out of the next paycheck.

To build a solid storm shelter, however, saving and investing must take top priority—and even more so in an uncertain economic climate. Proverbs 6:8 commends the hardworking ant, who "Provides her supplies in the summer, / And gathers her food in the harvest." Remember Joe, the pediatrician, from Chapter 6? He and his wife made a commitment to save money. By saving instead of spending, they have watched their resources—and their financial security—grow.

> **The best decision makers are those who have developed a sound investment philosophy on which to base their choices.**

- Secular Mythconception: Get rich quick.
- Strategic Truth: Get rich slow.

After pumping gas into his car, a friend of mine recently stood in a convenience-store checkout line for more than ten minutes just to pay for the purchase. Why the wait? The Georgia lottery jackpot had just hit ten million dollars, and the store was jammed with would-be winners jostling to purchase tickets. Everyone wants to get rich quick. One young man I know spends five dollars per week on lotto tickets. Not long ago he won a fourteen-dollar payoff. He was elated and, I suspect, more determined than ever to keep playing in pursuit of "the big one."

Consider, though, what that young man could do instead by investing his five dollars each week. Even at a (relatively low) 5 percent interest rate, his money would grow to $1,476 in just five years. And in forty-eight years, when the fellow was ready to retire, he would have $52,054.

Proverbs 21:5 says, "The plans of the diligent lead surely to plenty, / But those of everyone who is hasty, surely to poverty." From an economic standpoint, it makes no sense to pursue long-shot odds in a hurry-up effort to get rich when there is a guaranteed—albeit slower—way to make money.

> It makes no sense to pursue long-shot odds in a hurry-up effort to get rich when there is a guaranteed—albeit slower—way to make money.

- Secular Mythconception: Time is an enemy.
- Strategic Truth: Time is an ally.

Watching today's investors is like watching an old "Beat the Clock" game-show rerun. Thinking that time is short, people scurry around looking for the "best" investment options since every day that passes is one less day available for wealth accumulation. Too often, such anxiety-driven decisions turn out to be poor ones. Harrison is a dermatologist I know. The short-term mind-set that once drove him to buy a big house, join an expensive country club, and generally go for life's "gusto" has come back to haunt him. Burdened by debt and with no preparations made for his children's education or his retirement, Harrison is in a race against time. He waited too long to start investing for the future, and like those who allow themselves to be pressured into hasty and ill-considered decisions, he now sees time as an enemy.

Had Harrison adopted a long-term outlook, time would have become his ally. Time is a tool—and the more you have of it, the better. It does not matter whether you have a lot of money to invest or just a little as long as you are willing to let time work on your behalf. For example, both a ten-thousand-dollar one-time investment and a one-hundred-dollar-per-month savings effort can yield significant rewards, thanks to the "magic" of compounding over time (see fig. 9.1 and fig. 9.2).

Time is a tool—and the more you have of it, the better.

- Secular Mythconception: Expect upward trends.
- Strategic Truth: Expect cycles.

Market cycles—the highs and the lows—should be expected.

People purchase stocks in the hope or belief that the stock price will go up. In our dogged attempts to ride the upward trends, any investment loss generally comes as an unwelcome surprise.

In reality, however, market cycles—the highs and the lows—should be expected. In more than forty years of tracking the performance of stocks and bonds, investment professionals have made one thing clear: What goes up must come down, and vice versa (see fig. 9.3).

The Magic of Compounding

Saving $10,000 Lump-Sum Deposit Will Grow in 30 Years To . . .

5%	$43,219
10%	$174,494
15%	$662,118
20%	$2,373,763

Figure 9.1

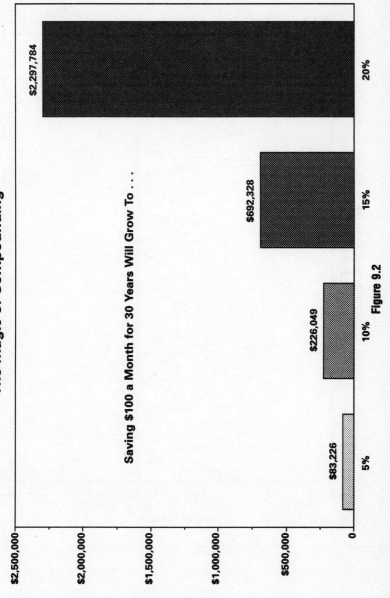

The Magic of Compounding

Saving $100 a Month for 30 Years Will Grow To . . .

$2,297,784 — 20%

$692,328 — 15%

$226,049 — 10%

$83,226 — 5%

Figure 9.2

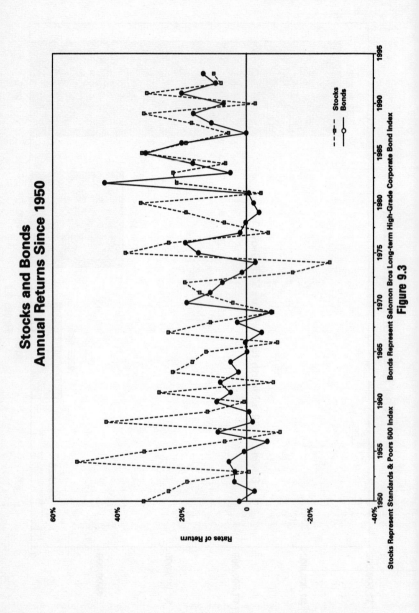

Stocks and Bonds
Annual Returns Since 1950

Figure 9.3

Stocks Represent Standards & Poors 500 Index   Bonds Represent Salomon Bros Long-term High-Grade Corporate Bond Index

The cycles experienced by stocks and bonds characterize every investment, from money markets to real estate. Such ups and downs would make perfect sense to King Solomon, who referred to a "day of prosperity" and a "day of adversity" (Eccles. 7:14) and wrote that there is a time for everything—from mourning to dancing (see Eccles. 3:1, 4). As investors, we must be prepared for both scenarios.

- Secular Mythconception: Time the market.
- Strategic Truth: Diversify your assets.

Biblical wisdom encourages a diversification of assets.

One of the most common investment strategies pursued by today's investors is market timing. The hope is that, with the proper combination of guesswork, maneuvering, and luck, the investor can "beat the system" and make money fast. The idea is simply to buy low and sell high—a strategy that works well in theory but is actually impossible to put into consistent practice.

Instead of trying to time the market, biblical wisdom encourages a diversification of assets. We ought to divide our assets into seven or eight portions, says Ecclesiastes 11:1–2, since we "do not know what [disaster] will be on the earth." As an investment strategy, asset diversification succeeds where market timing fails. Again, we will explore this concept in greater detail in the chapters to come.

PINPOINTING YOUR PERSONAL PARADIGM

A paradigm reflects the assumptions and biases that determine how you will interpret any given experience. As such, your paradigm influences your perspective. From a financial standpoint, two common paradigms drive most investment decisions: the paradigm of hoarding and the paradigm of effective investing. The mythconceptions described in the last section commonly manifest themselves in a hoarding mentality. On the other hand, operating from a paradigm shaped by strategic truths allows for effective investing. Also, because the strategic truths are rooted in biblical wisdom, the effective investor recognizes that God owns it all and that He is in control. The result of this perspective is investment freedom.

The effective investor recognizes that God owns it all and that He is in control.

Which one are you—the hoarder or the effective investor? One way to accurately assess your personal paradigm is to measure how it affects your decision-making process. Hoarders and effective investors are marked by two very different mind-sets:

The Hoarder	The Effective Investor
Reactive	Proactive
Blind	Visionary

Are You Reactive or Proactive?

I know a man named Peter who invested in a start-up company that became phenomenally successful. Within months, Peter saw his initial investment jump 450 times in value. Shortly thereafter, though, the stock price plummeted, and Peter's investment was only worth 100 times its original value. Most investors would be overjoyed with this net gain, yet all Peter could see was the loss. Gripped by fear, Peter began hoarding his wealth, hoping against hope for an upturn in the price of his stock—which he now monitors almost constantly.

Peter is a reactive investor. His emotions—and his investment decisions—are driven by market fluctuations. Proactive investors, on the other hand, expect market highs and lows. They are content to monitor their investments on a monthly, or even quarterly, basis. With an effective investment strategy in place, they take responsibility for their decisions and do not fall victim to fear or the temptation to blame others for their losses.

Are you like Peter? Take the following quiz to measure your reactive or proactive position. Be honest with yourself and circle the number, 1 to 5, that best reflects how much you disagree (1) or agree (5) with each statement. (Note: This test and others in this chapter are not meant to peg you with a "right" or "wrong" label. Rather, you can use your scores as simple indicators of where your paradigm lies and then consider whether you need to make a paradigm shift.)

If an investment drops in value, I have a hard time giving or spending any money; instead, I want to hang on to what I have left.	1 2 3 4 5
I check my investment positions weekly, if not daily, so I will know when to make a move.	1 2 3 4 5
I tend to blame others—my broker, my spouse, other investors—for my market losses.	1 2 3 4 5
I get nervous "riding" the market; when stock prices start to dip I want to jump ship.	1 2 3 4 5
I cannot predict the future, so I watch the market fluctuations for investment clues and make my decisions accordingly.	1 2 3 4 5

Total your score: _____

5–11 Your proactive approach will go far toward making you an effective investor.

12–17 You are in the neutral zone. Watch for more clues to determine your personal paradigm.

18–25 Your reactive tendencies may make you lean toward the hoarding mentality.

Whether your approach to investing is reactive or proactive is a good paradigm indicator. Equally telling is your ability—or lack thereof—to identify sound investments by accurately assessing the risks and rewards involved.

Are You Blind or Visionary?

Once there was a man who, before embarking on a long journey, called together his servants and entrusted his assets to them. One servant received about five thousand dollars, another got about two thousand, and the third was given just over one thousand.

While their master was gone, the first two servants invested so as to double their money. The third fellow, however, was afraid to take any chances. Digging a hole, he hid his one thousand dollars safely in the ground.

When the master returned and discovered what had happened, he praised and promoted the two money-making men. The third servant, though, found himself stripped of his resources and his responsibilities, for in his master's eyes he was wicked, lazy, and just plain stupid. This story, found in Matthew 25:14–30, illustrates two investment outlooks. The visionary investor deftly balances risks and rewards to identify worthy investment opportunities. The blind investor, on the other hand, is crippled by the fear of undertaking even a small degree of risk, choosing instead to hoard his limited assets where he thinks they will be safe. Blindness can also strike in the form of an inability to see any risk. Throwing caution to the wind, the blind investor may plunge headlong into any investment that promises a payoff—from shrimp futures to Brazilian opal mines.

Are you visionary or blind? Consider this test a financial eye examination:

I am only interested in "guaranteed" investment deals.	1 2 3 4 5
I am apt to follow a "hot tip" if it sounds like a big moneymaker.	1 2 3 4 5
I like to keep my money in the bank or in relatively secure money-market funds.	1 2 3 4 5
Brazilian opal mines sound good to me; after all, long odds offer the biggest payoff.	1 2 3 4 5
I tend to view an investment as either "risky" or "rewarding," but not both.	1 2 3 4 5

Total your score: _____

5–11 You probably have the vision necessary for effective investing.

12–17 Invest with caution, taking care to weigh all risks and rewards.

18–25 Stay away from the market—at least until you get a good pair of eyeglasses!

Every investor falls into one of two categories: You are either accumulating wealth or working to preserve it. Neither phase benefits from a hoarding paradigm. The best investors use their proactive and visionary abilities to plot and follow a strategic course to financial success.

THE ACCUMULATION AND PRESERVATION OF WEALTH

Joe, the pediatrician, is not financially independent. He and his wife are pursuing many financial goals—including setting aside the funds necessary to educate their four young children. Remember Judy's Aunt Avis, from Chapter 3? By the time she retired, thanks to her chosen lifestyle, she had achieved financial independence. With no one to support, her chief financial concern was investing her nest egg so she could continue to live comfortably.

Joe is in the accumulation phase. He needs to save money and invest it in order to achieve his long-term financial goals. Aunt Avis, on the other hand, was concerned with preservation. She had reached most of her financial goals and needed to concentrate on protecting the purchasing power of her investments.

You need an investment strategy.

The two investors represent different financial phases, but their investment objectives are remarkably similar. Both the wealth accumulator and the preserver want to see their investments grow, protect themselves against financial loss, and be sure that they have enough money to meet their individual needs and goals. Whether you are an accumulator or a preserver, a beginning investor or a seasoned pro, your objectives are probably no different than those shared by Joe and Aunt Avis. You need to make wise decisions to preserve and grow your resources. You need an investment strategy.

SIX STEPS TO EFFECTIVE INVESTING

Our firm has clients in both the accumulation and preservation phases. We have developed a Sequential Investment Strategy to address their individual financial needs. This approach, outlined in figure 9.4, includes six steps that work at any income level. And no matter which financial phase you are currently in, you can use this strategy to achieve both your immediate and lifetime goals.

Sequential Investing

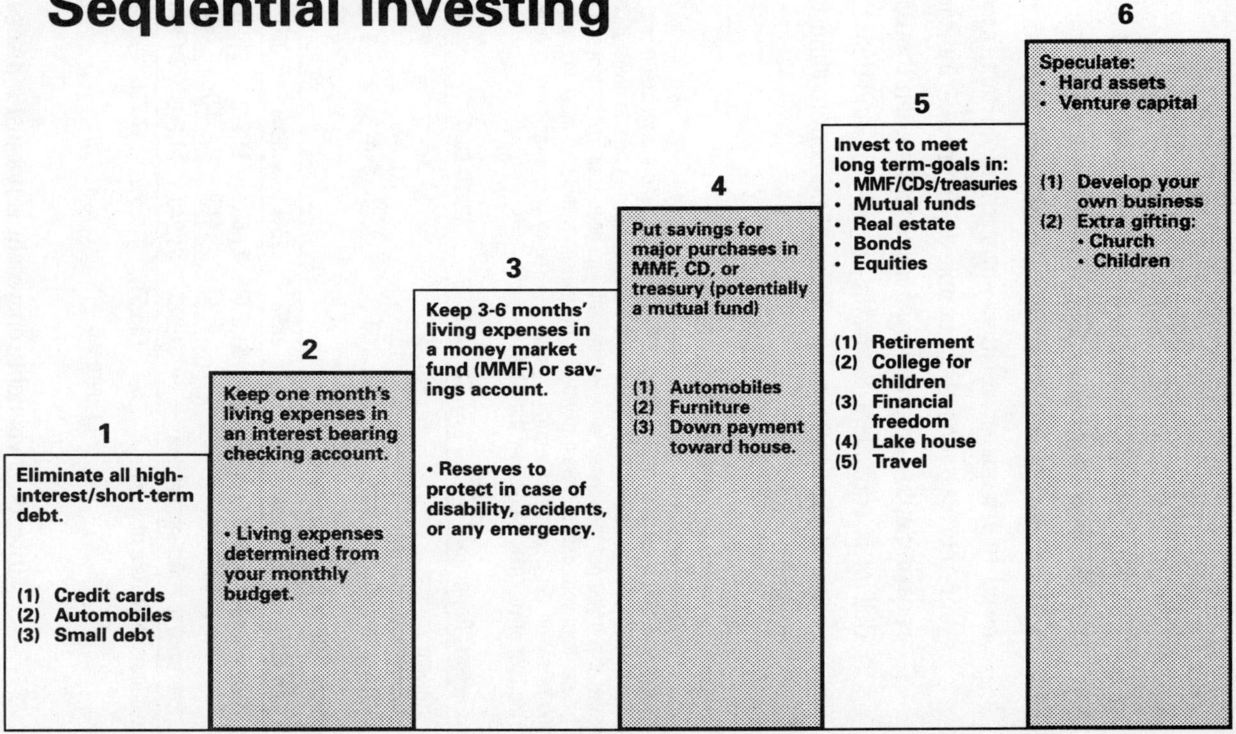

1

Eliminate all high-interest/short-term debt.

(1) Credit cards
(2) Automobiles
(3) Small debt

2

Keep one month's living expenses in an interest bearing checking account.

• Living expenses determined from your monthly budget.

3

Keep 3-6 months' living expenses in a money market fund (MMF) or savings account.

• Reserves to protect in case of disability, accidents, or any emergency.

4

Put savings for major purchases in MMF, CD, or treasury (potentially a mutual fund)

(1) Automobiles
(2) Furniture
(3) Down payment toward house.

5

Invest to meet long term-goals in:
• MMF/CDs/treasuries
• Mutual funds
• Real estate
• Bonds
• Equities

(1) Retirement
(2) College for children
(3) Financial freedom
(4) Lake house
(5) Travel

6

Speculate:
• Hard assets
• Venture capital

(1) Develop your own business
(2) Extra gifting:
  • Church
  • Children

Figure 9.4

Step One: Eliminate all high-interest debt.

The best investment you can make is to get rid of all high-interest, short-term debt. Pay off credit-card balances and automobile and other installment loans, even money owed to friends or relatives—everything, in fact, except your mortgage. As the example in figure 9.5 indicates, repaying auto and credit-card loans totaling ten thousand dollars is equivalent to making a ten-thousand-dollar investment earning anywhere from 15 percent to almost 20 percent:

Is It Wise to Pay Off Debt?

Assume that you have a car loan on which you still owe $7,000 and a bank credit card on which you owe $3,000. You saved $10,000 and now are considering how to invest it. Remember that if you put the money in an investment, you need your investment's return to be greater than your debt's interest payments; otherwise, it would be wiser to use the $10,000 to pay off the debt. What return would be required by your investment in order to offset the cost of your debt? Consider the tables below.

Annual Interest Payments:	Car Loan		Credit Card		Total
Amount you owe	$7,000	+	$3,000	=	$10,000
Interest rate charged	10.0%		18.0%		
Interest due after one year	$ 700	+	$ 540	=	$ 1,240

Investment Rate of Return Options:				
Your Marginal Tax Bracket:	20%	25%	30%	35%
Return needed on $10,000	$1,550	$1,653	$1,772	$1,908
Taxes due on earnings	(310)	(413)	(532)	(668)
Net return to equal interest due	$1,240	$1,240	$1,240	$1,240
Required Investment Rate of Return	15.5%	16.5%	17.7%	19.1%

Figure 9.5

"Investing" via debt repayment is not just a means to garner a high rate of return. It is also 100 percent guaranteed; your investment cannot "go sour." You will not find any stockbrokers offering such a risk-free—and truly golden—opportunity!

Step Two: Keep one month's living expenses in an interest-bearing checking account.

Once you have repaid all high-interest debt, begin funneling your available cash into an interest-bearing checking account. Review your spending plan (see Chapter 6) to find out how much money you need, on average, each month. Use the checking account as a savings vehicle for accumulating the cash equivalent of one month's living expenses.

Liquidity is important at this stage. The money in this account must be readily available to meet the cost of minor emergencies—from car or home repairs to relatively inexpensive medical needs.

> **The best investment you can make is to get rid of all high-interest, short-term debt**

Step Three: Keep three to six months' living expenses in a money-market fund or savings account.

Major emergencies—from the loss of a job to an unexpected medical crisis—need not spell disaster. Once you have one month's expenses earning interest in a checking account, save for major emergencies via a money-market fund or a savings account.

Having three to six months' living expenses stashed in a liquid investment vehicle allows you to "be your own bank." The ability to "borrow" from your own savings ensures your financial survival in the face of an unforeseen calamity. Think such misfortune could never be your lot? As Matthew 5:45 reminds us, God

> **Having three to six months' living expenses stashed in a liquid investment vehicle allows you to "be your own bank."**

"makes His sun rise on the evil and on the good, and sends rain on the just and on the unjust."

One final note: The easy accessibility of money-market and savings-account funds can create the temptation to overspend. Discipline yourself not to touch this money; left alone, your "emergency-only" savings will grow nicely.

Step Four: Save for major purchases in a bank CD, government-security mutual fund, or treasury bill.

Step four opens the door to the traditional world of investing. Bank certificates of deposit, government funds, and treasury bills are all conservative, low-risk investments—ideal savings vehicles for purchases such as cars, furniture, and even the down payment on a home.

How much money you choose to keep invested in such conservative investments depends on your individual needs. In general, though, I recommend a goal of at least five thousand dollars. Also, your investments should mature within five years; such a short time horizon enables you to withdraw funds as needed without incurring penalties. As the amount within each fund grows, stagger maturity dates so you have access to part of your resources while the rest continues to earn interest.

Step Five: Invest to meet long-term goals.

Refer to the goals you established in Chapter 5. Investing for long-term goals—such as a college education, increased giving, or financial independence—calls for a diversified investment portfolio. Money-market funds, mutual funds, real estate, bonds, and international equities may all be part of your picture. Chapters 10 and 11 will help you tailor your portfolio to meet your individual needs—including your financial goals, your investment time line, and your personal tolerance for risk.

One long-term goal shared by most investors is home ownership. Just as step one described how debt repayment offers a lucrative investment vehicle to beginning investors, so should paying off a mortgage appeal to investors who have reached step five. By making payments toward the outstanding principal over and above your regular monthly mortgage payments, you can significantly decrease the amount you would normally lose to interest (see fig. 9.6 and fig. 9.7).

> **Speculation must be pursued responsibly and only after steps one through five have been completed and all financial goals are met.**

Step Six: Speculate.

As the Sequential Investment Strategy Illustration on page 171 shows, steps one through four are stages in the accumulation phase. Steps five and six pertain to the preservation of wealth. No one wants to lose money; speculation, therefore, must be pursued responsibly and only after steps one through five have been completed and all financial goals are met.

The term *speculation* typically conjures up images of "throwaway money," but in my opinion, there is no such thing. Speculation—investing in hard assets, tax shelters, venture capital, and the like—carries a significant amount of risk. It also demands time and a willingness to become actively involved with the investments themselves. The next two chapters will help you determine whether speculation should play a role in your overall financial strategy.

Paying Off Your Home Mortgage

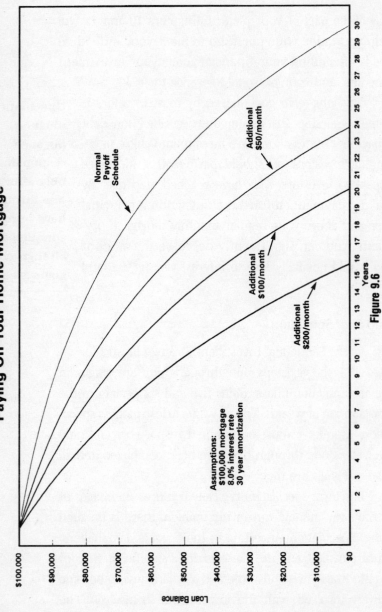

Assumptions:
$100,000 mortgage
8.0% interest rate
30 year amortization

Normal Payoff Schedule

Additional $50/month

Additional $100/month

Additional $200/month

Loan Balance

Years

Figure 9.6

Paying Off Your Mortgage Early

Payment Options:	Total Principal Payments	Total Interest Payments	Total of All Payments	Years to Retire Mortgage
Normal Payment Schedule	$100,000	$164,155	$264,155	30.0
Additional $50 to principal per month	100,000	124,246	224,246	23.9
Additional $100 to principal per month	100,000	101,695	201,695	20.2
Additional $200 to principal per month	100,000	75,891	175,891	15.8

Figure 9.7

PRACTICING YOUR PARADIGM

Every year our firm hears from about a thousand people peddling "surefire" investment strategies, "terrific" deals, and "golden" opportunities. Not once has someone approached us saying, "Hey—let me show you a really bad deal."

Every investment looks good at the outset. In reality, however, only a select few turn out to be as solid or profitable as projected. With the right paradigm and a well-mapped investment strategy, though, you can learn to spot the truly good deals and determine whether they fit into your personal financial plan.

Someone once said the anxiety that often accompanies stock-market and other investing is "just part of the game," and that those who win are those who can "take it." I do not believe that. For one thing, anxiety should not play a role in your investment decisions. For another, investing is not a game.

When To Bui built his southern California house, he was not playing a game. His visionary outlook motivated him to accept the risk of fire and build accordingly. His neighbors, however, focused only on the financial rewards

> **Every investment looks good at the outset.**

> **Anxiety should not play a role in your investment decisions. Investing is not a game.**

of less expensive housing, failing to recognize—or pretending not to see—the danger.

To Bui was also proactive. His responsible planning allowed him to weather the firestorm. Others, watching the flames engulf their lives, could only react in anguish and despair and resolve to do it right when they rebuilt their homes.

In the final chapters of this book I want to equip you to build as To Bui did. You will learn how to do it right. By accurately measuring your personal tolerance for risk, and discovering how to diversify your assets to meet your individual goals, you can construct a financial shelter that will stand up to any storm.

10

Step 7: Balance Risk and Reward

One of my goals, as I mentioned in Chapter 5, was to learn to snow ski by age fifty. I'm happy to say I reached that goal, and today few vacations hold as much appeal as a ski trip taken with my family and friends.

Judy, however, did not share my zeal for skiing. Ever the good sport, she graciously endured the ski lessons I pressed on her, but she would have much preferred spending her time on the beach. I desperately wanted Judy to catch my "ski fever," and I began to think about the factors that influenced our very different outlooks. I realized that, to me, skiing offered tremendous rewards, while Judy eyed the sport as a series of unappealing risks. Here's how I sorted them out:

Ron's Rewards	Judy's Risks
1. Time spent with family	1. Time spent freezing to death
2. Fun exercise	2. Unwanted work and effort
3. New hobby	3. One more thing to have to do
4. Conquer a mountain	4. Fall down and break something
5. Sense of achievement	5. Sense of failure

As the day drew near for our second family ski trip, I grew increasingly excited. Judy was apprehensive, and remembering my mental list of our different rewards and risks, I resolved not to pressure her to ski. When we reached the slopes, though, Judy surprised me. Teaming up with our daughter Cynthia, she spent a day conquering the beginner slopes—and discovered that skiing really could be fun.

Afterward, I shared my risk-reward breakdown with Judy. She agreed that the risks associated with skiing had, in her mind, far outweighed any potential rewards. The success of her recent experience, however, gave rise to a whole new set of rewards that suddenly outpaced the risks:

Analyzing risks and rewards pits our fears against our desires and clarifies the decision-making process.

Judy's Rewards

1. Being with the family
2. Laughing at yourself and others
3. Conquering something new
4. Enjoying God's creation
5. Sharing in the fun

This story illustrates the daily risk-reward balancing act we all must perform. When a young fellow asks a girl out for dinner, the reward of a date outweighs the risk of rejection. Successful dieters are those for whom the risk of being overweight eclipses the reward of giving in to their high-calorie cravings. Even young children may stack the rewards of raiding the cookie jar against the risk of punishment if they are caught.

Analyzing risks and rewards pits our fears against

our desires and clarifies the decision-making process. A correct assessment of potential risk may motivate us to get off the ground or ensure that we do not venture too far out on a limb. And finally, a good balancing act enables us to maximize our rewards while minimizing the risks involved. This goal, graphed in figure 10.1, represents an investor's ultimate challenge:

The Investor's Challenge

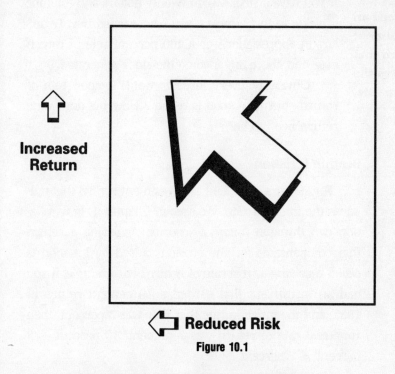

Increased Return

Reduced Risk

Figure 10.1

RECOGNIZING THE REWARDS

People invest in order to reap a reward. Many investments—such as buying into a company or purchasing bonds to fund specific projects—carry "feel-good" benefits. Rewards like these, though, are difficult to quantify. Instead, we generally measure an investment according to its rate of return: an investment's yield plus its appreciation—that is, the income it generates plus its growth in value. Income is earned through things like interest, dividends, and rental payments. It is paid on a regular basis—typically monthly, quarterly, or annually.

Income is fairly predictable; appreciation is not. If you have a stock worth twenty dollars and it jumps in value to forty dollars, you have earned twenty dollars in appreciation—or a 100 percent rate of return over and above any income the stock generated.

You need an investment return that outpaces the inflation rate.

Obviously, every investor wants a good rate of return—but how good is "good"? How big does your return need to be?

Beating Inflation

For starters, you need an investment return that outpaces the inflation rate. We saw, in Chapter 1, how inflation can threaten financial security. Achieving a return that compensates for the erosion caused by inflation is called receiving a "real rate of return." For example, if you had an investment that earned a 10 percent return in 1993, and the inflation rate that year was 3 percent, then your real rate of return was 7 percent: 10 percent − 3 percent = 7 percent.

Historically, certain investments have beaten inflation more often than others. Figure 10.2 illustrates how stocks, bonds, and treasury bills have fared against inflation since 1920.

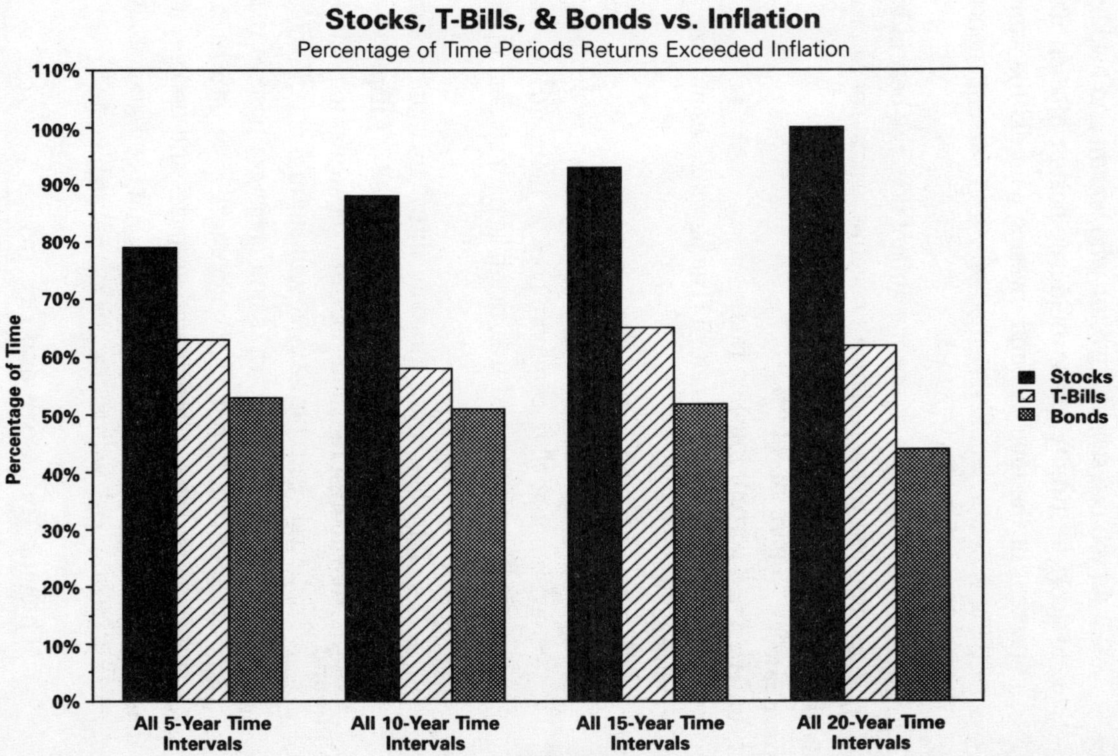

Stocks, T-Bills, & Bonds vs. Inflation
Percentage of Time Periods Returns Exceeded Inflation
Percentage of Time
110%
100%
90%
80%
70%
60%
50%
40%
30%
20%
10%
0%
All 5-Year Time Intervals
All 10-Year Time Intervals
All 15-Year Time Intervals
All 20-Year Time Intervals
Stocks
T-Bills
Bonds

Figure 10.2

As you can see, an investor who bought and held on to stocks for twenty years would have beaten inflation 100 percent of the time. A bond investor who did the same thing, however, would have had only a 44 percent chance of beating inflation.

Of course, if your investment does not beat inflation you will experience a negative real rate of return:

Inflation is not the only threat to your rate of return.

5 percent return

−6 percent inflation rate

(1%) real rate of return (The parentheses indicate a negative total.)

In any given year, achieving a negative real rate of return is not at all uncommon. Look at figure 10.3 to see how stocks, bonds, and treasury bills have stacked up to inflation since 1950.

You can beat inflation and still not have enough money to pursue your goals and dreams.

Inflation is not the only threat to your rate of return. Other economic risks discussed in Chapter 1—from interest rate and stock-market swings to political upheaval—can chip away at your storm shelter. To help clients handle these risks and achieve a positive real rate of return, our firm encourages asset diversification. By mixing investment strategies and options, as you will see in the next chapter, you can significantly reduce risk without sacrificing reward.

Achieving Your Goals and Dreams

You can beat inflation and still not have enough money to pursue your goals and dreams. Refer to the goals you established in Chapter 5. How much money do you need? How much time do you have? What rate of return

Nominal & Real Rates of Return

Year	Inflation Rate	Stocks		Bonds		Treasury Bills	
		Nominal Return	Real Return	Nominal Return	Real Return	Nominal Return	Real Return
1950	5.8%	31.7%	25.9%	2.1%	−3.7%	1.2%	−4.6%
1951	5.9	24.0	18.1	−2.7	−8.6	1.5	−4.4
1952	0.9	18.4	17.5	3.5	2.6	1.7	0.8
1953	0.6	−1.0	−1.6	3.4	2.8	1.8	1.2
1954	−0.5	52.6	53.1	5.4	5.9	0.9	1.4
1955	0.4	31.5	31.1	0.5	0.1	1.6	1.2
1956	2.9	6.6	3.7	−6.8	−9.7	2.5	−0.4
1957	3.0	−10.8	−13.8	8.7	5.7	3.2	0.2
1958	1.8	43.4	41.6	−2.2	−4.0	1.5	−0.3
1959	1.5	12.0	10.5	−1.0	−2.5	3.0	1.5
1960	1.5	0.5	−1.0	9.1	7.6	2.7	1.2
1961	0.7	26.9	26.2	4.8	4.1	2.1	1.4
1962	1.2	−8.7	−9.9	7.9	6.7	2.7	1.5
1963	1.7	22.8	21.1	2.2	0.5	3.1	1.4
1964	1.2	16.5	15.3	4.8	3.6	3.5	2.3
1965	1.9	12.5	10.6	−0.5	−2.4	3.9	2.0
1966	3.3	−10.0	−13.3	0.2	−3.1	4.8	1.5
1967	3.0	24.0	21.0	−5.0	−8.0	4.2	1.2
1968	4.7	11.1	6.4	2.6	−2.1	5.2	0.5
1969	6.1	−8.5	−14.6	−8.1	−14.2	6.6	0.5
1970	5.5	4.0	−1.5	18.4	12.9	6.5	1.0
1971	3.4	14.3	10.9	11.0	7.6	4.4	1.0
1972	3.4	19.0	15.6	7.3	3.9	3.8	0.4
1973	8.8	−14.7	−23.5	1.1	−7.7	6.9	−1.9
1974	12.2	−26.5	−38.7	−3.1	−15.3	8.0	−4.2
1975	7.0	37.2	30.2	14.6	7.6	5.8	−1.2
1976	4.8	23.8	19.0	18.6	13.8	5.1	0.3
1977	6.8	−7.2	−14.0	1.7	−5.1	5.1	−1.7
1978	9.0	6.6	−2.4	−0.1	−9.1	7.2	−1.8
1979	13.3	18.4	5.1	4.2	−9.1	10.4	−2.9
1980	12.4	32.4	20.0	−2.6	−15.0	11.3	−1.1
1981	8.9	−4.9	−13.8	−1.0	−9.9	14.7	5.8
1982	3.9	21.4	17.5	43.8	39.9	10.5	6.6
1983	3.8	22.5	18.7	4.7	0.9	8.8	5.0
1984	4.0	6.3	2.3	16.4	12.4	9.8	5.8
1985	3.8	32.2	28.4	30.9	27.1	7.7	3.9
1986	1.1	18.5	17.4	19.8	18.7	6.1	5.0
1987	4.4	5.2	0.8	−0.3	−4.7	5.5	1.1
1988	4.4	16.8	12.4	10.7	6.3	6.4	2.0
1989	4.6	31.5	26.9	16.2	11.6	8.4	3.8
1990	6.1	−3.2	−9.3	6.8	0.7	7.8	1.7
1991	3.1	30.5	27.4	19.9	16.8	5.6	2.5
1992	3.0	7.7	4.7	9.4	6.4	3.5	0.5
1993	3.0	10.0	7.0	13.2	10.2	2.9	−0.1
Average	4.3%	13.6%	9.3%	6.6%	2.3%	5.2%	0.9%

Figure 10.3

do your investments have to earn in order for you to fulfill your goals and dreams?

Suppose you want to pay for your child's college education. Public Television's "Wall Street Week" puts the present cost of four years at a private college at $100,000 to $150,000. Of course, public-supported schools can be much less expensive—although Janet Bodnar, author of *Kiplinger's Money-Smart Kids*, predicts that by the year 2011, public tuition could run as high as $130,000.

Let's say you decide you need $100,000. So far, though, you have only managed to save $10,000. The good news is that your child is only three years old—meaning you have fifteen years to come up with the money.

Time really is money. According to figures 10.4 and 10.5, you could grow your $10,000 to $92,655 in fifteen years if you earned a 16 percent rate of return. Or, you could invest $1,000 per year over that same fifteen years and hit $100,815—but you would need to earn a 24 percent return.

Of course, you could lower your required rate of return by investing more money at the outset. Investing $3,000 per year instead of only $1,000, for example, would mean you would only need an 8 percent return to reach $100,815.

Likewise, as the old saying goes, time really is money. Your $1,000 invested each year at 8 percent may not add up to much in fifteen years ($27,152), but if you had thirty years in which to invest, you would more than reach your $100,000 goal. According to the chart, you would wind up with $113,283. If you are investing to meet a specific goal—be it funding your child's education or wedding, or your own retirement—remember that the earlier you get started, the lower your rate of return needs to be.

The rate of return you require in order to meet your financial goals represents your investment reward. Harder to quantify—but no less significant—is the amount of risk you are willing to accept.

REALIZING THE RISKS

An investment's risk is defined as its *volatility.*

Suppose you purchased two different stocks for $100, and after five years, both were worth $200. During that time, the price of the first stock had bounced from a $20 low to a $300 high. The second stock's price fluctuated between $150 and $250. Even though both stocks wound up at the same point, the first stock, with its wild price swings, was more volatile. Since you do not know when you may be forced to sell an investment, any investment that carries more volatility than another is considered the riskier of the two.

The earlier you get started, the lower your rate of return needs to be.

Many people view investments in black-and-white terms: Either an investment is risky or it is not. In reality, though, investments may be grouped in a range of risk categories based on their historical volatility:

Very High Risk: Junk bonds, speculative stocks, futures, options

High Risk: Corporate bonds, growth stocks, rental real estate

Moderate Risk: U.S. Treasury and high-rated municipal bonds, blue-chip stocks

Low Risk: Savings accounts, money-market funds, CDs

COMPOUNDING
TIME + MONEY + YIELD

Investing a Lump Sum of $10,000

Time in years:

Yield:	5 years	10 years	15 years	20 years	25 years	30 years	35 years	40 years
2%	$11,041	$12,190	$13,459	$14,859	$16,406	$18,114	$19,999	$22,080
4%	12,167	14,802	18,009	21,911	26,658	32,434	39,460	48,010
6%	13,382	17,908	23,966	32,071	42,919	57,435	76,861	102,857
8%	14,693	21,589	31,722	46,610	68,485	100,627	147,853	217,245
10%	16,105	25,937	41,772	67,275	108,347	174,494	281,024	452,593
12%	17,623	31,058	54,736	96,463	170,001	299,599	527,996	930,510
14%	19,254	37,072	71,379	137,435	264,619	509,502	981,002	1,888,835
16%	21,003	44,114	92,655	194,608	408,742	858,499	1,803,141	3,787,212
18%	22,878	52,338	119,737	273,930	626,686	1,433,706	3,279,973	7,503,783
20%	24,883	61,917	154,070	383,376	953,962	2,373,763	5,906,682	14,697,716
22%	27,027	73,046	197,423	533,576	1,442,101	3,897,579	10,534,018	28,470,378
24%	29,316	85,944	251,956	738,641	2,165,420	6,348,199	18,610,540	54,559,126
25%	30,518	93,132	284,217	867,362	2,646,978	8,077,936	24,651,903	75,231,613

Figure 10.4

END OF YEAR VALUES

Investing $1,000 Each Year

Time in years:

Yield:	5 years	10 years	15 years	20 years	25 years	30 years	35 years	40 years
2%	$5,204	$10,950	$17,293	$24,297	$32,030	$40,568	$49,994	$60,402
4%	5,416	12,006	20,024	29,778	41,646	56,085	73,652	95,026
6%	5,637	13,181	23,276	36,786	54,865	79,058	111,435	154,762
8%	5,867	14,487	27,152	45,762	73,106	113,283	172,317	259,057
10%	6,105	15,937	31,772	57,275	98,347	164,494	271,024	442,593
12%	6,353	17,549	37,280	72,052	133,334	241,333	431,663	767,091
14%	6,610	19,337	43,842	91,025	181,871	356,787	693,573	1,342,025
16%	6,877	21,321	51,660	115,380	249,214	530,312	1,120,713	2,360,757
18%	7,154	23,521	60,965	146,628	342,603	790,948	1,816,652	4,163,213
20%	7,442	25,959	72,035	186,688	471,981	1,181,882	2,948,341	7,343,858
22%	7,740	28,657	85,192	237,989	650,955	1,767,081	4,783,645	12,936,535
24%	8,048	31,643	100,815	303,601	898,092	2,640,916	7,750,225	22,728,803
25%	8,207	33,253	109,687	342,945	1,054,791	3,227,174	9,856,761	30,088,655

Figure 10.5

In addition to the amount of volatility an investment carries, there are also several different types of risk that can affect an investment's performance. You need not be an investments expert; by simply understanding that these risks exist, you can occasionally minimize their impact on your holdings.

Market (Systematic) Risk

Market risk represents the traditional definition of risk. It is the degree to which the market, as a whole, is volatile. If the president of the United States is reported to have had a heart attack, investment markets react— whether or not the report is true. Any event or economic trend that makes investors fearful or anxious will be reflected in a market downturn.

Unsystematic Risk

Unsystematic risk pertains to the risk associated with a specific investment. The value of a company's stock, for example, rests on any number of factors, from how well the company is managed to what the competition is doing to public perception of the company's success. Likewise, bond values may vary in relation to the company or municipality's creditworthiness, and real estate prices rise and fall according to factors ranging from the local economy to how well the property is managed.

Interest-Rate Risk

Interest-rate risk is the risk associated with how a change in interest rates will affect an investment's return. If you own a corporate bond earning 8 percent, and interest rates jump to 10 percent, your bond will lose value in the face of the newer, 10 percent bonds. Stocks, too, are affected by interest rates; when interest rates rise, stock prices generally fall as investors seek greater returns with less risk outside the stock market.

Currency Risk

Currency risk affects international investments as the value of the U.S. dollar rises and falls in relation to the currency of a given country. If the dollar goes up in value, the worth of a stock or bond of a company based in that country will decline, and vice versa.

Today's sophisticated investors typically invest a significant portion of their portfolio internationally.

After World War II, more than two-thirds of the world's investable assets (stocks and bonds) were found in the United States. By 1990, though, only 33 percent were in U.S.-based companies. Today's sophisticated investors typically invest a significant portion of their portfolio internationally, either through direct purchase of a company's stocks or bonds, or via a mutual fund.

HOW MUCH RISK CAN YOU HANDLE?

Given such a wide range of investment risks—in both amount and type—calculating how much volatility you are willing to accept can become a confusing process. To help our clients discover their personal tolerance for risk, we have developed an Investor Profile Questionnaire. The results from this questionnaire will enable you to tailor your investment strategy to meet your personal needs and style.

Circle the number associated with the response that best describes your response to each statement, and then total the circled numbers for each section.

Investor Profile Questionnaire

	Strongly Agree	Agree	Neutral	Disagree	Strongly Disagree
Return Requirements: I am most interested in earning a high long-term rate of return that will allow my portfolio to grow faster than the inflation rate.	4	3	2	1	0
Risk Tolerance: I am willing to tolerate sharp up and down swings in the return on my portfolio with the expectation of a higher return than a more stable investment would generate.	4	3	2	1	0
Time Horizon: My major investment goals are primarily long-term (i.e., greater than 10 years).	4	3	2	1	0
Tax Considerations: I would prefer an investment that provides an opportunity to defer taxation of appreciation and income to future years.	4	3	2	1	0
Liquidity Requirements: I am financially able to accept a low level of liquidity (i.e. cash & liquid assets) in my investment portfolio.	4	3	2	1	0
Income Requirements: I do not require a high level of current income from my investment portfolio.	4	3	2	1	0
Capital Protection: I am willing to risk a short-term loss of principal in return for a potentially higher long-term rate of return.	4	3	2	1	0

Based on your total, you can determine what type of investor you are and what sort of an investment portfolio you require:

Point Ranges:
- 0–10   Conservative
- 11–20   Moderate
- Over 20   Aggressive

BALANCING RISK AND REWARD

Are you a conservative, moderate, or aggressive investor? In general terms, the conservative investor pursues a low-risk/low-return strategy. The moderate investor follows a moderate-risk/moderate-return strategy. And the aggressive investor adopts a high-risk/high-return strategy.

To change either side of the equation requires a balancing act. For example, if aggressive investors want to reduce their level of risk, they must be willing to give up some of the reward potential as well. Likewise, if conservative investors need a higher rate of return in order to meet a financial goal, they must be willing to take on additional risk.

This give-and-take process reflects a basic investment principle. Many investors, however, are unwilling to accept the limits inherent in the risk-return trade-off. Often—and especially during times of economic uncertainty—people try to "beat the system" by pursuing an alternative investment strategy. Too often, though, the approach they choose is a mistake.

> **Balancing risk and reward is a give-and-take process that reflects a basic investment principle.**

FOUR COMMON INVESTMENT MISTAKES

1. The Market-Timing Myth

Every investor knows the secret to stock-market success: Buy low and sell high. The trouble is, nobody can consistently time investment moves to make this strategy work. There is no formula for market-timing magic.

Even so, for the investor who works with a short time horizon, the lure of what could happen under the buy-low-sell-high scenario is often irresistible. A jump in the price of a particular stock creates a "had I but known" mind-set, leaving the investor drooling over the potential discovery of the next "great timing" opportunity.

In truth, though, the notion of outguessing the system is nothing more than an arrogant dream. Market turning points are almost always determined by unprecedented events such as Federal Reserve interest rate shifts or unanticipated economic events. Moreover, market gains typically occur in quick bursts. Figure 10.6 demonstrates what would happen if you missed investing in only the best nine months of the stock market over thirty years.

The notion of outguessing the system is nothing more than an arrogant dream.

In a thirty-year period, could you spot the nine months that would make a difference? If you missed them, your return would be no greater than that afforded by T-bills. But, by investing in stocks, you would face significantly more risk.

One final problem is the taxes you must pay on any gains you earn. Every time you buy and sell, you must first make up the money you lost to taxes—about 28 percent these days—before you can even begin to pursue a profit.

2. The Past-Performance Pitfall

There is no guarantee an investment that once performed well will continue to do so.

Many people pick investments simply because they have been profitable in the past—even though there is no guarantee an investment that once performed well will continue to do so. Likewise, in selecting a financial adviser, a common temptation is to choose the person or management firm that has performed best in the past. The problem with this logic is that it is reactive rather than proactive. Also, the very thing that worked in your favor last year will probably work against you this year.

The Frank Russell Company, one of the nation's leading pension-fund consultants, studied the performance of

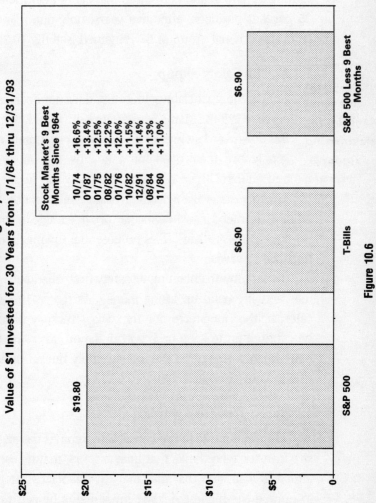

The Market Timing Myth
Value of $1 Invested for 30 Years from 1/1/64 thru 12/31/93

Stock Market's 9 Best Months Since 1964	
10/74	+16.6%
01/87	+13.4%
01/75	+12.5%
08/82	+12.2%
01/76	+12.0%
10/82	+11.5%
12/91	+11.4%
08/84	+11.3%
11/80	+11.0%

S&P 500 — $19.80

T-Bills — $6.90

S&P 500 Less 9 Best Months — $6.90

Figure 10.6

the top 25 percent of institutional grade managers—the folks who manage funds for the biggest and best companies. After two years, only three managers held their top 25 percent positions; after five years, only one manager from the original group of 62 remained (see fig. 10.7).

3. The Safety Slipup

Conservatism offers no potential for maximizing financial rewards.

In the financial world, safety does not necessarily equal wisdom. Many conservative investors, fearing the downward swings of an uncertain economic market, ignore their need for a healthy rate of return and squirrel their resources away in the least-risky investments available. U.S. Treasury bills, bonds, and other guaranteed investments may provide a safe harbor—yet such conservatism offers no potential for maximizing financial rewards.

In fact, by maintaining a "safety-first" mentality, you may actually wind up losing money. As figure 10.8 indicates, neither long-term nor thirty-day treasury bills can be counted on to keep pace with inflation. Knowing this, how much worse off is the money safely buried under a tree in your backyard!

4. The Aggressive Agenda

On the flip side of the conservative coin is the aggressive investor who thinks that time is short, that he cannot afford to wait, and that the smartest financial strategy is to pursue the highest-yielding investments he can find—regardless of the risk involved.

If I told you that investment A would earn a 30 percent return in the first year while investment B would garner only 5 percent, your investment preference would be obvious. But what if I told you that in the second year, investment A would lose 20 percent while B continued to grow at 5 percent? Which alternative, then, ought you to choose?

Without studying the actual numbers, most folks would naturally gravitate toward investment A. After all, the logic goes, if you make 30 percent in one year, you can afford to lose some the next. In reality, however, investment B—the slow and steady grower—represents a better choice. Do the math with me:

Investment	Year One	Year Two
A. $100	× 30% = $130 ×	−20% = $104
B. $100	× 5% = $105 ×	5% = $110.25

With investment B, by allowing compounding to work for you, you will actually earn about two-and-a-half-times more money than you would by speculating on the high-yield (and highly volatile) investment A.

DOING IT RIGHT

As investment strategies, none of these approaches— from market timing to ultra-aggressive investing—will consistently enable you to achieve a real rate of return. As Judy was before she discovered the joys and rewards of skiing, you will always be hindered by an unnecessary level of risk.

In the chapter to come you will learn how to ride what is called the "efficient frontier." By selecting investment portfolios that maximize rewards while pinpointing

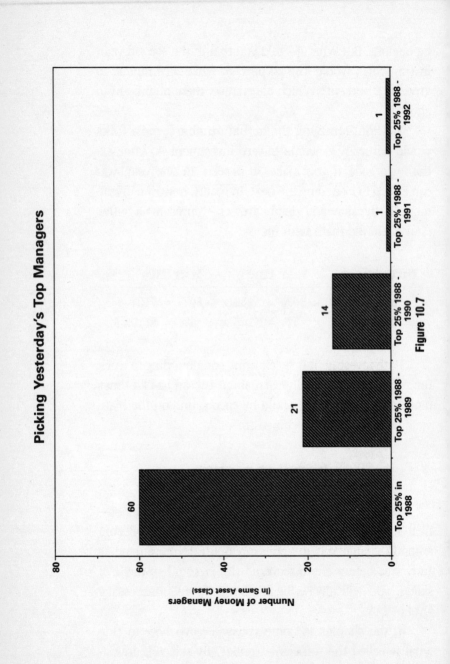

Picking Yesterday's Top Managers

Number of Money Managers (In Same Asset Class)

Top 25% in 1988	60
Top 25% 1988 - 1989	21
Top 25% 1988 - 1990	14
Top 25% 1988 - 1991	1
Top 25% 1988 - 1992	1

Figure 10.7

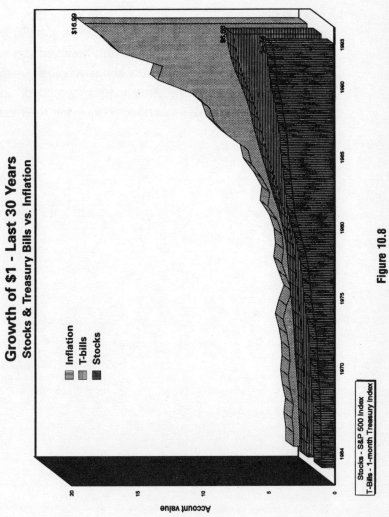

Growth of $1 - Last 30 Years

Stocks & Treasury Bills vs. Inflation

Inflation
T-bills
Stocks

$16.99

$6.58

Account value

1964   1970   1975   1980   1985   1990   1993

Stocks - S&P 500 Index
T-Bills - 1-month Treasury Index

Figure 10.8

the minimum amount of necessary risk, your storm shelter will provide the financial protection you need to meet your goals.

Investing, like skiing, can be awkward, humiliating, and frustrating. When you do it right, however, you will enjoy the rewards—both financial and psychological—that come with a job well done. And, as your investment skills improve, you can look forward to conquering the mountain.

Step 8:
Diversify Your Portfolio

In my first accounting job I had a client named Alfred whose tax return was the lengthiest and most complex I have ever seen. It was the 1970s, and Alfred consistently made more than a million dollars per year. I was stunned, therefore, when he told me he needed to declare bankruptcy.

Alfred was wealthy, but he had made one critical investment mistake. He had put all of his money into one condominium project in a city that had seen a booming real estate market. When the market suddenly soured, Alfred lost virtually everything he owned.

I wish I had known then what I know today. It is never wise, as the old saying goes, to put all of your eggs in one basket. I was not then a financial planner, but perhaps—had I better understood the whys and how-to's of diversification—I could have helped Alfred construct a better storm shelter.

Unlike Alfred, you now have the tools you need to build and fortify your own storm shelter. In everything from taking your financial physical to balancing invest-

> **You now have the tools you need to build and fortify your own storm shelter.**

ment risks and rewards, you have used the best "brick and lumber" the Bible—and the wisdom of experience— have to offer. Now, by applying what you have learned and diversifying your assets, you can find your place on the "efficient frontier"—the point at which you incur the absolute minimum amount of risk for the return you receive.

DIVERSIFICATION: A STRATEGY THAT WORKS

Diversification is spreading your money among different types of investments. By doing so, you diminish your overall risk.

A retired couple wanted to start a small business in the mountains of North Carolina. They were leaning toward opening a cozy gourmet coffee shop when a friend intervened. The coffee shop, he pointed out, would be a welcome retreat from the brisk autumn breezes and winter snows, but sales were apt to be sluggish during the hot summer months.

Rethinking their plan, the couple decided to open a coffee and ice cream shop. If coffee sales lagged in the heat, the promise of ice cream would lure the summertime crowds. Similarly, a hot cup of coffee would keep the winter customers coming even if ice cream sales melted. By diversifying their offerings, the couple had hit upon a plan that would reduce their overall risk while enhancing their total return.

This strategy works with equal success in the investment world. Figure 11.1 demonstrates what happens to a dollar invested in company A, company B, and in a 50–50 mix over five years.

| Years | Company A Stock | | Company B Stock | | Company C Stock | |
	Return	Market Value	Return	Market Value	Return	Market Value
Original Investment		$1.00		$1.00		$1.00
1	−5.0%	0.95	20.0%	1.20	7.5%	1.08
2	25.0%	1.19	−5.0%	1.14	10.0%	1.18
3	−10.0%	1.07	35.0%	1.54	12.5%	1.33
4	10.0%	1.18	15.0%	1.77	12.5%	1.50
5	30.0%	1.53	−15.0%	1.50	7.5%	1.61
Average Return	10.0%		10.0%		10.0%	

Figure 11.1

As you can see, after five years the stock in company A is worth $1.53. During the same time, company B's stock rose to $1.50. But with 50 cents invested in both companies, the investor would have $1.61. And not only would the investment be worth more, the risk would be decreased: Both company A and company B experienced two years of negative returns, but the mixed investment always earned a positive rate of return.

Illustrated, a diversification strategy might look something like figure 11.2, in which an initial investment of $100,000 is made in one lump sum and then spread out over five different investments.

THE DIVERSIFICATION SEQUENCE

A portfolio is a group of individual investments. When our firm helps a client structure his or her investment portfolio, we follow a sequential strategy that includes diversification among several categories (see fig. 11.3).

By moving from one category to the next, this approach gives an investor the ability to diversify within diversification, thereby strengthening the total portfolio.

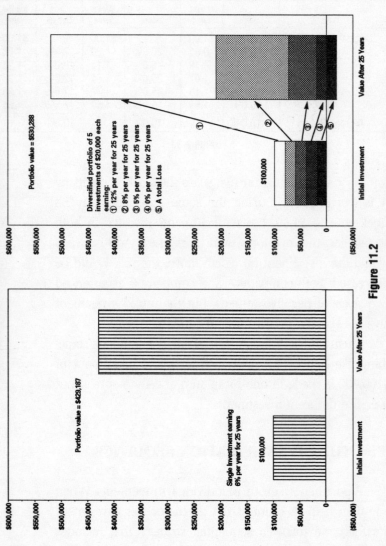

Figure 11.2

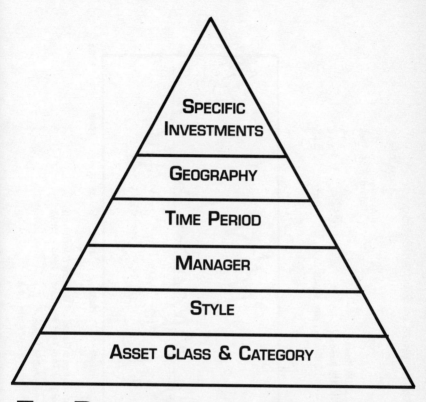

THE DIVERSIFICATION HIERARCHY

Figure 11.3

Diversification by Asset Class and Category

Diversification by asset class is the most widely practiced form of diversification. It involves combining many different assets—such as stocks, bonds, international investments, and real estate—into a single portfolio. Because these various assets have different risk and return characteristics, they rise and fall in value independent of one another. By combining two or more asset classes, as figure 11.4 illustrates, you can reduce the volatility, or risk, in the portfolio.

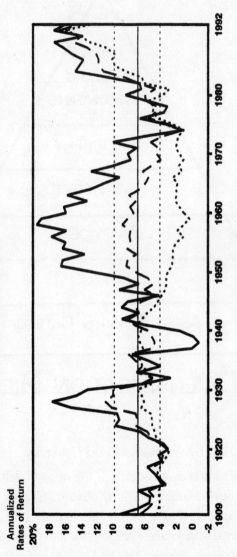

The Benefits of Diversification

1900 - 1993

	Average Return	Risk
US Stocks	9.3%	5.1%
US Bonds	4.7%	3.1%
40% Stocks / 60% Bonds	6.9%	2.8%

Annualized Rates of Return (Nominal)
Rolling Ten-Year Periods: 1900 - 1992

Figure 11.4

Source: Frank Russell Company "Capital Market History"

Asset categories are a subgroup of asset classes. A smart diversification strategy includes investments in different categories within each asset class. This chart highlights asset classes and categories, and offers some common examples in each category:

Asset Class	Category	Example
Stocks	Large Company	Dow Jones Industrials Blue Chips
	Small Company	NASDAQ, Speculative
International	Developed Markets	Japan, Great Britain, France
	Emerging/Developing Markets	Mexico, Chile, Singapore, Thailand
Bonds	Government	Treasury Notes/Bills, Series EE
	Corporate	Bonds, Debentures
	Municipal	Airport Authority, County Revenue & Sales Tax
	Speculative	Junk, International, Mortgage
	Mortgage Pools	GNMA, FNMA
Real Estate	Income-Producing	Apartment Complex, Building Space
	Non–Income-Producing	Raw Land
	Stocks	REITs
Precious Metals	Gold and Silver	Kruggerands, Coins, Bars
Cash	Cash/Cash Equivalent	Money-Market Fund, Bank CDs
(Note: When you begin to build your own portfolio, the "cash" asset class will not be included in your asset allocation. Your cash positions must be maintained in liquid investments to cover living expenses and any emergencies that might arise.)		

Diversification by Investment Style

An investment style is the strategy used for buying and selling investments.

Value-driven investors look for stocks or bonds that are selling below their book value on the assumption that an undervalued stock price represents a good deal.

Growth investors evaluate stocks based on a company's quarterly earnings report. If a company shows consistently high earnings, a growth investor may see that as a good indicator of future value and growth.

Market-oriented investors take a broad economic view and choose stocks that are affected by interest rates, industry trends, and other market factors. Bank and construction-company stocks represent investments that may appeal to market-oriented investors.

A smart diversification strategy includes investments in different categories within each asset class.

Small capitalization, or *small cap*, investors look for relatively small companies that, because of their lower total market value, may escape the notice of stock analysts. Small cap investors hope to discover the next Microsoft.

The best-diversified portfolios incorporate a combination of two or more investment styles since, as the graphs in figure 11.5 illustrate, a style that was effective at one time may be less effective at another.

This comparison of styles applies only to stocks and bonds. In reality, there are as many styles of investing as there are investment managers, and each investment manager may have a basic style, but change it or fine-tune it to meet his or her own personality, experience, and objectives. Not only that, but there are different styles within different asset classes. The point is that different styles perform differently in various scenarios; therefore, diversification by manager style within asset classes is a further protection against risk of loss. Investing purely in one style, even if other diversification methods are used, will still expose you to unnecessary risks.

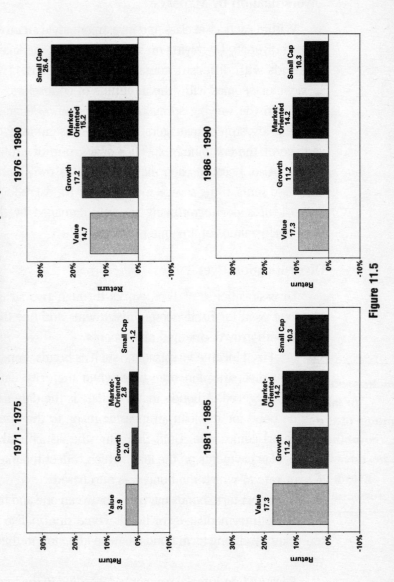

Comparison of Performance by Style

1976 - 1980

Value 14.7	Growth 17.2	Market-Oriented 15.2	Small Cap 26.4

1986 - 1990

Value 17.3	Growth 11.2	Market-Oriented 14.2	Small Cap 10.3

1971 - 1975

Value 3.9	Growth 2.0	Market-Oriented 2.8	Small Cap -1.2

1981 - 1985

Value 17.3	Growth 11.2	Market-Oriented 14.2	Small Cap 10.3

Figure 11.5

Diversification by Manager

Within each asset class and investment style an investor can diversify by relying on several different managers
(or funds with different managers). As Proverbs 11:14
says, victory comes with "the multitude of counselors."

Given the varying specializations and knowledge of
different investment managers, it makes sense to take advantage of the combined expertise of a group of professionals. Also, because each manager has his own biases
and blind spots, using several managers (or funds) reduces
the risk of a portfolio's being severely damaged by the
poor performance of any one individual.

Diversification Over Time

Diversification over time works through two strategies, one used for fixed-income investments and one that
works with growth-oriented investments.

Fixed-income investments, such as bonds, benefit
from diversification over time when maturity dates
are staggered. A bond's maturity date is the date that
the bond (or the loan an investor made to the bond-
issuer) comes due. Until that time the issuer makes
regular payments on the loan, which reflect the interest rate at which the bond was purchased.

Short-term bonds mature in between one and five
years. Intermediate-term bonds come due in five to
ten years. And long-term bonds mature after ten to thirty
years.

Because bonds make payments according to the interest rate at the time the bond was purchased, it is possible
to have a long-term bond that offers a much greater return

> It makes sense
> to take
> advantage of the
> combined
> expertise of a
> group of
> professionals.

than that which is currently available. A portfolio that includes bonds with staggered maturity dates takes advantage of the fact that as interest rates increase, assets will be available to purchase new bonds, and as interest rates decrease, existing bonds will outperform their newer counterparts.

Dollar-cost-averaging is the second time-diversification strategy. This technique, used to purchase stocks and mutual funds, offers an excellent way to invest on a periodic basis. Monthly savings, quarterly 401K investments, and annual IRA contributions can all be used to dollar-cost average.

Because the value of stocks and mutual funds fluctuates over time, it is impossible to pinpoint the best time to make a purchase. By staggering your purchases you can lower your risk of entering the market at a very high point. Instead, you pursue the average price.

Dollar-cost-averaging is the second time-diversification strategy.

The idea behind dollar-cost averaging is to invest a regular amount of money in a particular stock or mutual fund on a regular basis. This strategy allows you to ignore market swings and, over time, achieve an average rate of return. Figure 11.6 illustrates how dollar-cost-averaging works.

Diversification by Geography

Real estate represents an investment that can benefit from geographical diversification. My client Alfred might have avoided bankruptcy had he invested in more than one city's real estate market. Real estate investment trusts (REITs) pool assets in order to buy land or real estate projects in several cities or states.

International investments comprise another asset class that could and should be geographically diversified.

Diversification by Time Period: Dollar-Cost-Averaging

Month	Dollar Amount Invested	Price Per Share	Number of Shares Purchased	Cumulative Number of Shares	Market Value of Total Investment
January	$100.00	$25.00	4	4	$ 100.00
February	100.00	20.00	5	9	180.00
March	100.00	12.50	8	17	213.00
April	100.00	10.00	10	27	270.00
May	100.00	8.33	12	39	325.00
June	100.00	8.33	12	51	425.00
July	100.00	10.00	10	61	610.00
August	100.00	12.50	8	69	863.00
September	100.00	12.50	8	77	963.00
October	100.00	16.67	6	83	1,383.00
November	100.00	20.00	5	88	1,760.00
December	100.00	25.00	4	92	2,300.00

Summary	
Total dollars invested	$1,200.00
Total number of shares purchased	92
Average price paid per share	$13.04
Year-end market value of total investment	$2,300.00

Figure 11.6

Emerging markets, such as those in Mexico and Singapore, may offer excellent growth potential. Developed countries, such as Japan and Great Britain, offer market opportunities that are relatively insulated from some of the systematic risk that drives the U.S. markets.

Note: International investments are best pursued through a professional manager or mutual fund. Also, because of the volatile nature of some emerging markets, these funds should only be considered by investors with an aggressive risk tolerance.

Diversification by Specific Investments

The final layer of diversification pertains to how you purchase your investments. You will want to select and purchase some stocks, bonds, or real estate yourself on an individual basis. To achieve truly effective diversification, however, you need to incorporate several mutual funds into your portfolio. Mutual funds offer the advantages of professional management and are described in more detail in the next section of this chapter.

BUILDING YOUR OWN DIVERSIFIED PORTFOLIO

Obviously, diversification makes for more effective investing. Earlier in this chapter I referred to the "efficient frontier." The following graph illustrates this concept in showing how diversification works to reduce risk and enhance return. An all-bond portfolio carries a degree of risk that can be reduced with the inclusion of stocks, all the way up to a 40 percent stock, 60 percent bond mixture (see fig. 11.7).

The points plotted on this graph represent the points at which, for any given stock/bond portfolio mix, investors incur the minimum risk for the return they receive. By adding more diversification to the mix, the efficient frontier can be moved, further reducing the risk associated with a particular return. Figure 11.8 illustrates what happens when international stocks are added to the U.S. stocks and bonds portfolio.

Diversification works to reduce risk and enhance return.

Building a diversified portfolio is a three-step process that begins with an investment plan based on your financial goals and your individual tolerance for risk. Once you have this strategy mapped out, you can buy and sell investments to tailor your portfolio to reflect the plan. Finally, you need to monitor your holdings.

The Efficient Frontier
Stock & Bond Portfolios

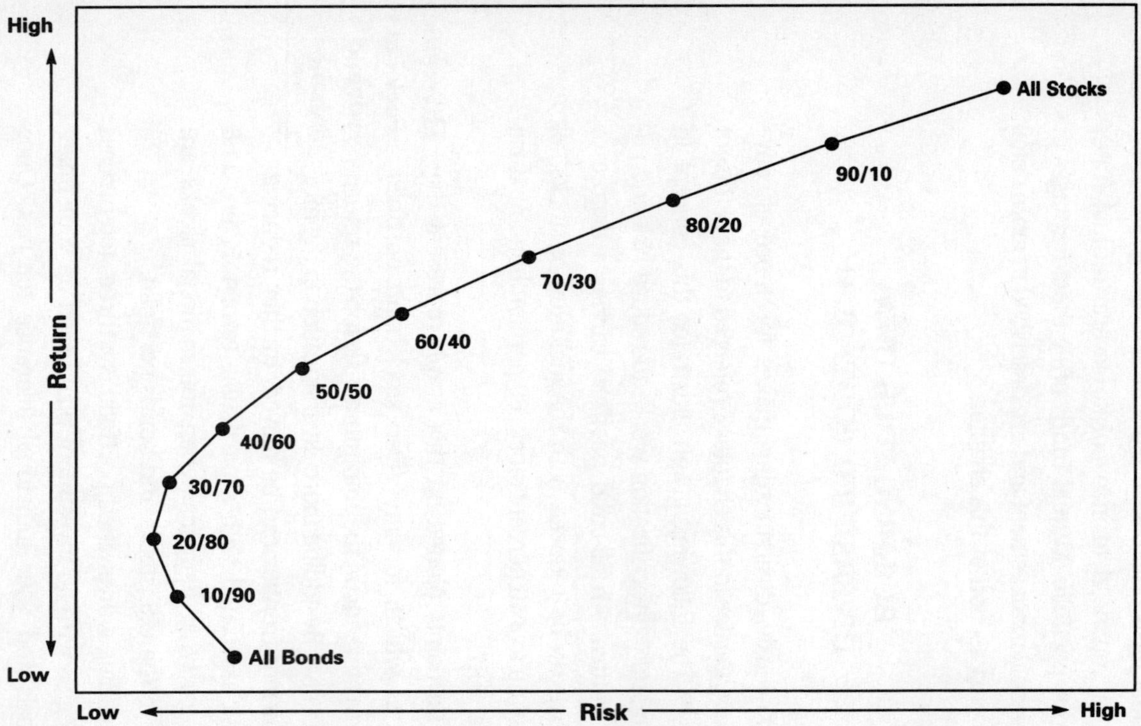

All Stocks

90/10

80/20

70/30

60/40

50/50

40/60

30/70

20/80

10/90

All Bonds

Return

High

Low

Risk

Low

High

Based on data from 1950 thru 1993

Figure 11.7

The Efficient Frontier
Non-U. S. Stocks, U. S. Stocks and U. S. Bonds

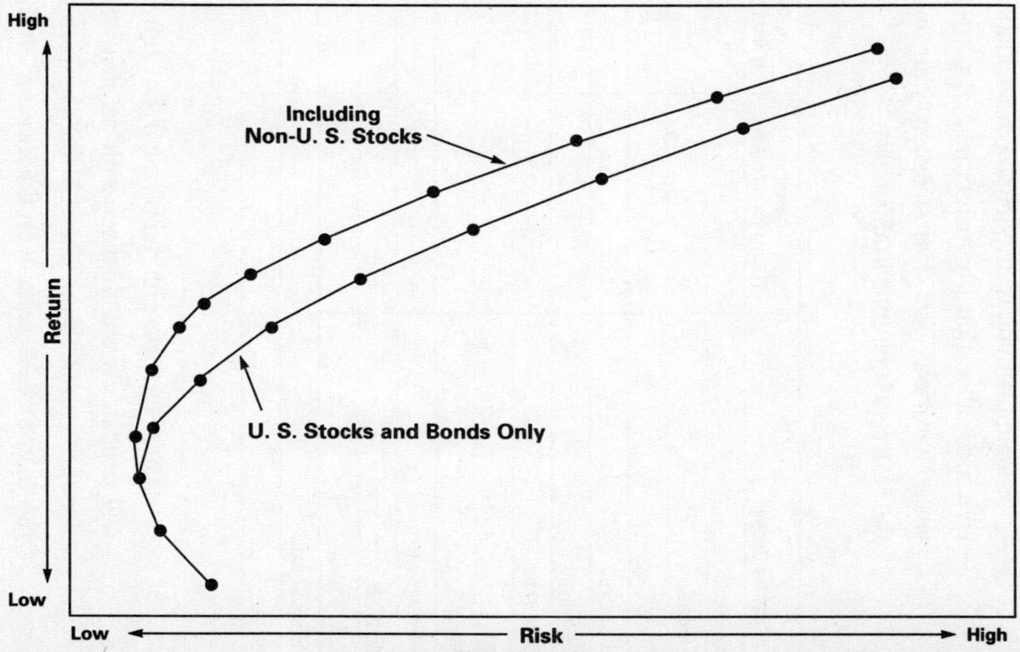

Including
Non-U. S. Stocks

U. S. Stocks and Bonds Only

Return

High — Low

Low — Risk — High

Figure 11.8

Step One: Make a Plan

Begin planning your portfolio by evaluating your current asset allocation (the percentage of your holdings invested in various asset classes). Record your findings under the "Current" columns in this chart:

Asset Class and Category	Current ($ Amt.) (% of Portfolio)	Desired Category ($ Amt.) (% of Portfolio)
U.S. Stocks		
Large Cap		
Small Cap		
Int'l Stocks		
Developed		
Developing		
Bonds		
Short-Term		
Intermediate		
Real Estate		
R.E. Stocks		
Precious Metals		
Total:		

Once you have entered your current information, you will probably want to meet with an investment professional to complete the chart. Using the results from the risk-tolerance assessment on the Investor Profile Questionnaire (see Chapter 10), you can establish a portfolio goal that complements your investment temperament.

Figure 11.9 illustrates how a portfolio might be structured, depending on the risk-tolerance level of a particular investor.

	Conservative	Moderate	Aggressive
U.S. Stocks			
Large Company	20%	25%	40%
Small Company		10%	20%
International Stocks			
Developed Markets	10%	10%	15%
Developing Markets		5%	10%
Bonds			
Short-Term	40%	20%	
Intermediate-Term	25%	20%	
Real Estate			
Real Estate Stocks		5%	10%
Precious Metals	5%	5%	5%
TOTAL	100%	100%	100%

Figure 11.9

Step Two: Buy and Sell

Once you have decided how to allocate assets for your investment portfolio, you may need to sell some of your current investments in order to reinvest the funds in a different asset and maintain your desired allocation percentages. As you look to invest, you may want to use a professional money management firm.

If you opt for the do-it-yourself approach to investing (and even if you contact an investment professional), there are several strategies and tools that you can use:

1. Mutual Funds. A mutual fund is a single investment in which an investor adds his or her money to that of other investors to create a pool of wealth that is professionally managed. Most mutual funds are comprised of twenty to one thousand stocks, bonds, or other investments, and require a minimum purchase of one thousand to five thousand dollars in fund shares.

In choosing a mutual fund, consider the fund's objectives. What type of securities will it include—stocks, bonds, or other investments? What type of investment style will the fund manager employ? Is the overall investment approach conservative, moderate, or aggressive? Do the fund's goals complement your own?

2. Investment Newsletters and Periodicals. There are almost as many investment analysts as there are investment strategies. Every adviser can make a convincing case to support his or her own outlook; what matters is whether the adviser's philosophy and goals match yours.

Sound Mind Investing, published by Austin Pryor, offers investment advice that, to me, appears biblically sound and professionally correct. By recommending specific portfolios and offering investment how-to's, *Sound Mind Investing* is both practical and personal. For more information, contact: Sound Mind Investing, P.O. Box 22128-R, Louisville, Kentucky 40252–0128 (The Reader services number is 502-426-7420).

3. Investment Clubs. An investment club is a group of investors who pool their resources to purchase stocks, bonds, and other investments. Typically, members attend regular meetings to discuss investment opportunities and one or two members of the group manage the fund.

Before joining an investment club, make sure you agree with the group's philosophy and goals. Like mutual

funds, investment clubs can offer reduced risk and increased return through diversification of assets—but you
incur the added risks of interpersonal conflict or potential
loss if a member of the group is forced to sell out prema-
turely.

Additional information on investment clubs may
be obtained from the National Association of Investors
Corporation (NAIC), which publishes the magazine
Better Investing. Contact NAIC at P.O. Box 220, Royal
Oak, Michigan 48068.

> **Rebalancing is
> one of the best
> ways to actually
> buy low and sell
> high.**

Step Three: Monitor

The third, and final, stage in building your portfolio
is monitoring. You should review your investment accounts on a monthly or quarterly basis. Remember that
your portfolio is structured according to a carefully developed plan. Market swings should not make you want to
buy or sell (unless you note a significant and continued
drop in one asset class or category). Also, your asset allocation percentages should remain constant, and you will
need to periodically rebalance your portfolio.

Rebalancing a portfolio involves simply noting where
growth and erosion have occurred and making correc-
tions. For example, suppose your asset allocation plan reflects a 65 percent stock/35 percent bond mix. If the stock
market improves and the bond market declines, however,
you may wind up at the end of one quarter with 72 percent of your assets in stocks and 28 percent in bonds.
Rebalancing means selling the extra 7 percent in stocks
and buying it back in bonds. (Interestingly enough, rebalancing is one of the best ways to actually buy low and sell
high!)

MAINTAINING THE
PROPER PERSPECTIVE

Diversification is the final step in designing and constructing a safe and secure storm shelter. In some ways, though, diversification is just the beginning.

Imagine a home built with a brick front, stucco sides, and vinyl siding on the back. Now add a roof that is part tin, part shingle, and part slate. Finally, enclose the whole thing with a fence that includes post-and-rail, picket, chain-link, and wrought-iron in a haphazard pattern. Does this house sound like one you would like to buy?

Probably not. Its inconsistency in design makes the house unappealing—and possibly unsafe as well. You would not want to live in such a ramshackle dwelling. Likewise, you would not want to rely on a piecemeal or randomly constructed financial storm shelter.

Throughout this book I have attempted to present building principles that are both biblically and practically correct. Just as you should not build a home with three different roofing materials, you cannot construct a storm shelter with anything other than consistent planning and materials. You cannot, for example, structure your spending plan along biblical guidelines and then create an investment portfolio based on a get-rich-quick mentality. The building blocks must complement one another if your storm shelter is to be weatherproof.

I hope that, through this book, I have challenged you to dismiss fear and anxiety from your construction crew. I hope that your blueprint now reflects some clearly defined goals and the means by which you can achieve them. Most of all, I hope I have encouraged you to take responsibility for your resources, trusting in a storm shelter that bears the mark of the Master Builder.

Epilogue

When I testified before the congressional subcommittee in 1992 the thought went through my mind that I was describing something so simple, surely everyone already knew it. Every time I have finished a book, I have felt the same way—surely everyone already knows and understands what I have just described; perhaps the readers will feel I have insulted their intelligence.

When these thoughts come, however, I remember some things that give me confidence: First, the best authors bring to life what others already know; they just express it in a way that reinforces shared beliefs and convictions. Second, I remember that our Lord Jesus did not make it difficult to understand the most important truth of all.

Also, I remember that effective communication is consistent and repetitive. If I have said things in this book that repeat my thoughts from other books it is because I believe we all need to be reminded that the things we ought to do are not difficult concepts. The eight steps described in Chapters 4–11 are the *what* to do. *How* to do it is not difficult either. This book has provided easily completed forms to guide you in doing what you need to do.

Why to do it is the motivation behind my writing this book. It is intended to help you survive and even thrive during uncertain economic times. If we do have uncertain economic times, which I believe we will, the Christian is the one who should be expected to not only survive but to thrive.

When to do it is your decision. You can begin now to do one or two things to get you started. This process will undoubtedly be different for each of you, but *the time to get started is right now*. The past cannot be retrieved; begin where you are and do all you can do.

I believe that the help you will require in doing this— and undoubtedly will receive—is spiritual help. As I have been thinking about this, I have also been meditating and praying about a certain portion of Scripture: Revelation 2 and 3, which contain the seven messages to the seven churches. The seventh message is to the church at Laodicea, and it says this:

> I know your works, that you are neither cold nor hot. I could wish you were cold or hot. So then, because you are lukewarm, and neither cold nor hot, I will vomit you out of My mouth. Because you say, "I am rich, have become wealthy, and have need of nothing"—and do not know that you are wretched, miserable, poor, blind, and naked—I counsel you to buy from Me gold refined in the fire, that you may be rich; and white garments, that you may be clothed, that the shame of your nakedness may not be

revealed; and anoint your eyes with eye salve,
that you may see. As many as I love, I rebuke
and chasten. Therefore be zealous and repent.

Lukewarmness happens when we believe we are
"rich, have become wealthy, and have need of nothing,"
when in fact we are "wretched, miserable, poor, blind, and
naked." In other words, when we have the wrong paradigm, when we believe we are self-sufficient and don't
need our Lord. His challenge to us is to come to Him in
repentance. When I first read this commandment to "be
zealous and repent," I wondered what the repentance was
from; now I believe it is repentance from self-sufficiency.

My concern in completing this book is that you suc-
cessfully heed the advice given here and consequently
believe you are self-sufficient. Unless you have the proper
paradigm of dependence and humility before our Lord,
all of your work will be for nothing.

We can't plan for what God is going to do in our
economy because we don't know what that is. We can,
however, be prepared for *whatever* He does by following
His principles, and the ultimate principle is dependence
on Him.

The verse that follows the passage quoted above is
very familiar. It is, "Behold, I stand at the door and knock.
If anyone hears My voice and opens the door, I will come
in to him and dine with him, and he with Me" (Rev. 3:20).
I believe Christ is saying to us, as Christians, "Don't be
self-sufficient; rather, be dependent upon Me. I am waiting
to invade your life so we can experience sweet fellowship
together." That sweet fellowship can occur under any eco-

nomic scenario. We can prepare for it by opening our hearts in dependence on Him.

If you do not know our Lord Jesus as your personal Savior, He is inviting you to open the door of your heart to Him. True security and significance come in knowing we have a relationship with the eternal God for all eternity. True security will never come through an investment portfolio or a financial plan. It can only come through a relationship with the eternal God.

Ron Blue
1100 Johnson Ferry Road NE
Suite 600
Atlanta, GA 30342
1-800-987-2987

STEPS TO PEACE WITH GOD

1. RECOGNIZE GOD'S PLAN—PEACE AND LIFE

The message you have read in this book stresses that God loves you and wants you to experience His peace and life.

The BIBLE says ... *"For God loved the world so much that He gave His only Son, so that everyone who believes in Him may not die but have eternal life." John 3:16*

2. REALIZE OUR PROBLEM—SEPARATION

People choose to disobey God and go their own way. This results in separation from God.

The BIBLE says ... *"Everyone has sinned and is far away from God's saving presence." Romans 3:23*

3. RESPOND TO GOD'S REMEDY—CROSS OF CHRIST

God sent His Son to bridge the gap. Christ did this by paying the penalty of our sins when He died on the cross and rose from the grave.

The BIBLE says ... *"But God has shown us how much He loves us—it was while we were still sinners that Christ died for us!" Romans 5:8*

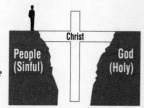

4. RECEIVE GOD'S SON—LORD AND SAVIOR

You cross the bridge into God's family when you ask Christ to come into your life.

The BIBLE says ... *"Some, however, did receive Him and believed in Him; so He gave them the right to become God's children." John 1:12*

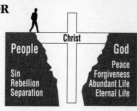

THE INVITATION IS TO:
REPENT (turn from your sins) and by faith RECEIVE Jesus Christ into your heart and life and follow Him in obedience as your Lord and Savior.

PRAYER OF COMMITMENT
"Lord Jesus, I know I am a sinner. I believe You died for my sins. Right now, I turn from my sins and open the door of my heart and life. I receive You as my personal Lord and Savior. Thank You for saving me now. Amen."

If you want further help in the decision you have made, write to:
Billy Graham Evangelistic Association, P.O. Box 779, Minneapolis, MN 55440-0779

If you are interested in options open to you regarding giving to the Lord's work through wills, gift annuities, trusts, and other gift programs, please contact us at the following address for your **free** information:

Billy Graham Evangelistic Association
Development Ministries
1300 Harmon Place
Minneapolis MN 55403

Telephone: (612) 338-0500
FAX: (612) 335-1244
Internet: http://www.graham-assn.org/bgeadev